WithInAsThru yoU!
The Handbook

A Handbook Best Experienced Self to self…

MIKE—

I DEDICATE THIS BOOK TO THE EVER INSPIRING POSSIBILITY YOU ARE. YOU WERE THERE FOR ME IN MOMENTS REMEMBERED. HERE'S TO YOU FULFILLING THE PROMISE ONLY YOU CAN FULFILL.

THANK YOU FOR BEING WHO YOU ARE.

APPRECIATED.

Scott

Av '08

WithInAsThru yoU!

This handbook,
This living consideration,
Is being passed from yoU to you,
Self to self,
As guide and journey companion.

IT has arrived
To offer simple processes to create
LIFE as you choose IT to BE.

IT has come
To give you
Back to Self.

Be then clear.
It's not intended to be your teacher!
Nor is it an answer to any of your questions.

IT IS,
In both form and function,
Your choice,
Arrived.

In form,
Written handbook.

In function,
A living consideration,
Withinasthru Self.

yoU to you.
Self to self,
Reader and Writer,
Written and Read,
One.

Its clearest gift,
Its most direct consideration...

Nothing in life happens to you.
Your life,
As you live IT,
Exactly as IT IS,
IS Occurring WithInAsThru yoU!

Your teacher, too,
Lives WithInAsThru yoU!

yoU
Are the one
You've been waiting for.

yoU
Are Answer
To every question
You'll ever
Ask.

With this consideration now before you...

Welcome back to Self!

—A. S. Kurslf

A. S. Kurslf Collaborative
1133 Broadway, Suite 706
New York, NY 10010

1-888-ASK-SELF
1-888-275-7353

COLLABORATORS

Inspiration:	Self
Co-Author:	yoU!
Co-Author:	Scott Kiere
Poet:	Ⴟ
Producer:	JeanMarie
Executive Producer:	Sarah E. Galewick
Editor:	Caress A. Kiere
Illustrator:	Scott Riddle
Layout:	R.E. Geddes
Advisor:	Warren Whitlock

Manufactured in the United States
ISBN: 978-1-934275-00-9

This handbook is dedicated to Self,
And to this part of Self,
that is you.

Thank you
for showing up!

Your willingness to be here
IS cause to celebrate.

Withinasthru Dedication & Celebration,

—A. S. Kurslf

Table of Contents

Eternal Gratitude...

To a mother who loved her son...
May she be ever sustained by her beautiful garden,
the return of her unconditional love expanded with grace.

To a father who gave freedom to a young boy,
a freedom which allowed him to become his own man.
May he live with peace knowing all is complete as is.

To a spouse who is infinite beauty and timeless muse...
May she ever know and feel her divine femininity
withinasthru her every movement through LIFE.

To two girls who reflect innocent joy...
May you forever know, be and live
love without conditions,
each in your unique melody,
dancing beep bop cool
to the beat of your own jazzy way.

To a project leader and producer who makes all things real...
May she live forever knowing the gift she is.

To an editor able to translate rainbow...
May she experience this process
as a mirror reflection of what exists within.

To an illustrator who captures visions with
Zen stroke flow...
May his work bring him ever beauty full expression.

To the designers whose magic gives life to words written...
May they design their lives with equal creativity and joy.

To one who was willingness enough to share
his conversation with God...
May he know, beyond any need to know whatsoever,
that his conversation made this one possible.

To a living steward of life's mystery school,
one of this time's truest avatars...
May her mythic life serve as inspiration
come home to every social artist's heart.

To a troubadour who lives as a spiritual peacemaker,
a most beloved community...
May his way of community reflect the peace in his heart.

To those committed
to transforming the way the world does business...
May your social venture continue
to network the world of commerce,
as catalyst for even more successful,
economically just and socially responsible
collaborations world-wide.

To every investor of resources...
May what is built together
sustain many
for many years to come.

To an advisor and a powerful promoter...
May all you've done to help make this project possible
circle as a boomerang bringing unimaginable wealth
to all areas of your life.

To a brother who exhales abundance and joy...
May you live into your hundreds,
such that you may receive at least a tenth of what you give.

To the coaches and mentors,
advisors and friends,
and every player and player's family who's contributed
in some small way...
May each know in own heart,
gratitude as certainty,
for the many gifts given along river's journey,
to where tigers hunt and dolphins swim.

To a sister who saw the possible long before it was seeable,
and a sister who brings gatherings into song and celebration...
May you both be able to receive Self seeing in return,
and may this seeing bring you ever happy tomorrows,
all that you deserve.

To an uncle whose 'captain my captain' way
inspired a young brother to ask clearer questions,
transforming gift of gab into poet's tongue...
May the clarity of his guidance be as relevant today
to those who seek, without asking,
his simple love, without conditions given.

To a legal expert evaluator like none other,
and a friend of lifetimes remembered...
May his heart be ever full
with the magic his way offers world.

To a cousin who so willingly assists...
May the richness you add to collaborations
fill your life and your home
with love by choice, knowingness and bliss.

To those who challenged and pushed,
who doubted and in moments even attacked...
May the wine of your inspiration to become more
live forever on your lips,
a toast and a smile to your long-life and well-being.

To a poet of ancient tongue who lives turtle's way...
May he find peace and fulfillment knowing
he elevated elephant presence into whale's song.

To the youth who speak and awaken withinasthru word...
May their voice be heard on LIFE's biggest stages.

To every poet, musician and artist
who ever moved, touched and inspired...
May your heart know the miracle you are,
as artist.

To those who have walked before,
who willingly chose Self...
May your legacies continue to guide all home to heart.

And to all fellow seekers and journeyers...
May you come to accept this inevitable moment,
living on purpose withinasthru passion,
LIFE as you choose IT to BE.

Ashea.

An Essential self-Introduction

7 July 2007

Dear Friend & Reader,

It's almost by accident that this handbook has arrived, at least in the form and voice that it's arrived. I say accident, perhaps, because I feel very excited by its coming forth and fortunate to have received it in the way I'm now sharing it with you. But really, even as I write this, I'm as surprised and humbled by what's arrived as anything I've ever experienced, so much so that I felt compelled to write this introduction. It's important that you know this handbook arrived through an extraordinarily ordinary guy.

I am the guy. My name is Scott. My friends know me as SK. I'm the one this handbook has arrived through. I say 'through' purposefully. I've not yet, by any stretch of my imagination, become a living example of the considerations in this handbook. Not by a long shot. Yet, this handbook has changed me. It's changed me indelibly. Because of it, I'm not the same brother who first engaged this project.

A change has occurred withinasthru me. A change I am both grateful to and for. A change I do intend to live and become, in my own way of applying the considerations and processes that have arrived. I hope that you'll receive as much benefit from this handbook as I have, because a truly powerful transformation has occurred in me through the process of writing this handbook.

I see LIFE, and my eternal connection to LIFE, as I've never seen it before. I listen to others and myself in ways I've never listened before. I now perceive the world in a way that seemed impossible for me to perceive, just a moment ago…a way that has increased my core fulfillment in being alive. A joy has filled my moments such that even when there are tears flowing down my cheeks, I feel joy. I see beauty just about everywhere. I love more deeply. I share more openly. I give and receive in harmonic reciprocity. In essence, I have become much more able to respond to this moment's occurrence powerfully and on purpose.

This transformation is so much more than I either anticipated or expected. And I invent the possibility that this transformation is absolutely possible for you, too, if you so desire it.

This is why I'm writing this self-introduction. This is why I'm now sharing my personal experience with you. I felt it necessary to pause in between edits to just sit and write to you so you know that this transformative experience, the process by which this handbook has arrived, is available to you, too, as you choose to really engage it.

It really is. If it weren't, it couldn't exist in any moment you are. I really get this idea now. I mean, just look, here you are in this inevitable moment where you now find yourself, here reading this handbook. How could it not somehow be a reflection of what lives too in your heart?

Perhaps, just perhaps, that's the utter simplicity of this entire consideration. Its simplicity is what excites me the most, because there is no real right or wrong way to read this handbook. It's just that it's so much more clearly experienced if you, like me, choose to read and experience it, Self to self.

What do I mean, "Self to self?" In many ways, this question is the "accident". "Who is Self?" is the core question I pursued as deeply as I've ever pursued a question before. Eventually, it was my absolute abandonment of everything I thought I knew that allowed me to become willingness enough to receive this handbook's living considerations. That's it. That's the essence of my shared process here. *This handbook was available only through my unknowing.* Everything I thought I knew often kept me stuck in moments without an exit. It was my unknowing that lead me into the richest experience of my life.

Through this process, I've come to experience Self as an *entelechy-Self* where entelechy is defined as a realization or actuality, as compared with a potentiality. Entelechy is a vital agent or force directing growth withinasthru life. And it's the essential ingredient to conscious evolution.

Your *entelechy-Self* then, is the *you* a million years from now—*you.* It's your smile in reflective transcendence where *you* have already become the living solution to every perceived problem you have today—had lifetimes ago—*you.* It's the *you* who has already become your every dream lived—*you.* This fully realized, or at least ever evolving self-realized *you* is your *entelechy-Self.*

This handbook, as best as I can possibly share in words, has been just this—**an experience withinasthru my** *entelechy-Self.*

What started as a deeper response to what I began in writing *WithInAsThru yoU! The Letters* transformed into this living consideration. My ability to claim full authorship disappeared the moment I was aware what had occurred. Because this handbook is so much more than what I could have ever written on my own. It's more than I could have ever written without you, the reader, as your smile truly did grace this process somehow. There is no clearer way for me to invite you into accepting that your arrival, as reader, absolutely helped this entire creative experience occur.

You see, something mystical occurred withinasthru me during the process of writing this handbook. Something that I had never experienced before. As I allowed myself to go deeper and deeper into the question, *Who is Self?*, I began to actually experience river as this inevitable moment. It was like a letting go, an allowing of some sort. A clearer presence became the moment itself, and with it, I became an increasingly subtle observer. The more I allowed this experience willingly, the more it arrived effervescently. The more I trusted and allowed it, the more willing I became to receive it. Ironically, or perhaps perfectly, the handbook arrived with very little effort from me at all. This is how I've come to understand the importance of both of our roles, reader and writer.

I've heard true sagas from authors of their process in writing a book. Metaphors from giving birth to backbreaking deadlines had kept me from simply writing for years. But when I truly engaged this process, it was almost effortless to me. I can honestly say that writing has become as much a new love as any I've ever known. And it's continually new. This is the gift I've received from this experience.

It is my hope that you'll experience a gift while reading it.

For it was in those light-filled voids of nothingness where I willingly traveled to the very root of my question, *Who is Self?*, that the question itself dissolved me—my identities, my roles, my very personality—into pure river flowing *entelechy-Self* experience. I began to get that this handbook really had nothing to do with me whatsoever. But I couldn't see that through my self-importance or my self-imposed limitations, because those were the very barriers to my receiving this experience.

It was my simple willingness to receive what I most desired that allowed this handbook's arrival. Yet, even as I share this thought, I'm reminded of a Taoist saying, "First enlightenment. Then, laundry."

It's important for me to communicate, as clearly as is possible, that I'm not here to claim enlightenment as who I am all the time. I'm no Guru. You need but ask my wife or children or anyone who knows me to quickly get that I'm as average a guy as they come.

As in any artistic endeavor, the end product was necessarily filtered by the artist. In this handbook, I am the filter. I've done my best to remain as clear as I know how throughout this process. However, please get that it's obviously filtered through me in ways you feel served by, as well as ways that perhaps clouded your reading experience. If the latter is true, please choose to be with the message, while discarding the messenger. Regardless, in a few very clear moments, I was willingness enough to ask for and receive more. This handbook is the result.

Writing this handbook has been the closest experience to what I imagine it's like for a great song to arrive via fingers on a piano keyboard or a sonnet written to reflect moonlight in a playwright's heart.

This is what this handbook most clearly reflects, to me. It's a living consideration arrived from *entelechy-Self* to me that I now share with you. And it's an experience that you too get to choose, if you will. Nothing more. Nothing less.

When I asked, "How may I most clearly re-present and share this *entelechy-Self* experience in such a way as to cause each reader to experience their own *entelechy-Self* withinasthru the very act of reading this handbook?", *A. S. Kurslf* was the name I was given. *A. S. Kurslf* is a direct invitation to everyone to Ask Self.

My clearest intention in presenting *WithInAsThru yoU! The Handbook* as a living consideration by *A. S. Kurslf* is to invite you to choose to willingly allow your own *entelechy-Self* experience and to express it. Then, to share it.

My truest invitation to you is this: **Will you choose to be willingness enough to read and receive this handbook as your own living experience, arrived from your *entelechy-Self*?**

Self to self. Regardless, may your journey be as you most clearly desire.

In Open Humility, Transparent Process & Grounded Invitation…

A Friend & Journey Companion,

sk

ps. Please share your experience of this handbook with me at *http://www.WithInAsThru.com*. Ashea.

Who is A. S. Kurslf?

(pronounced A. S. cure self)

A. S. Kurslf
IS
a living invitation for you to know,
not hope or merely believe,
but to know withinasthru experience,
you've been the answer
to every question
you've ever asked.

Ask then Self,
as your every question
emerges from the depths
of pure BEing.

And be willingness enough
to become a Living Answer
to each question you ask.

WithInAsThru yoU!

A. S. Kurslf

as poet,
a voice arrived,
intercedent come,
to spiral new possibilities
into existence...

When invited,
able to bend light waves
into river's current,
mountain wisdom
to ocean's reception,
folding whale song intention
from lifetimes experience,
pure poetic form ...

Words,
so often worth,
a thousand pictures or more...

Scott ⚡ Kiere

a simple brother,
extraordinarily ordinary,
willingness enough
to allow this process
withinasthru
contributions to the
A. S. Kurslf Collaborative,
as fulfillment
to a promise and a choice
to live on purpose,
reminding,
even as he's remembering…

We Are All One!

Opening Considerations

As with anything in life, it is important to remember that you get what you give. Giving and receiving are eternal energetic circles. They are forever in connected collaboration and magnetic equilibrium.

To this end, the following are a few considerations or experiments, between you and your Self, for you to play with during the course of your journey withinasthru this handbook.

Nothing offered here is a "have-to" on this journey. Instead, choose to see them as "get-to" choices you can make as you will. As you so choose, you'll come to know you're receiving the most value from this resource, as per your own experience.

Each consideration is offered for the purpose of your truest fulfillment, expressed and experienced, and is worthy of your sincere consideration and playful experimentation.

Consider, if you will:

- Nothing in this handbook is either true or false except by which you feel and experience IT to BE so. This is the most important part of your process here. Please honor IT. Be true to what's true for you, yes?

- Make a conscious choice to really get involved with this handbook. Engage IT, read IT, reread IT, BE with IT, laugh with IT and cry with IT, and by all means have fun with IT in as many ways as is possible. The more fun you have with your participation and experimentation, the more easily you'll travel a lifetime's worth of transformation within comparative moments.

- See IT as a mirror reflection of your Self in a new form and function. AND be gentle with yourself as you come to see that you are THAT you are. The process back to Self-realization IS as you choose IT to BE. Be, then, as gentle as a river flowing, flexible as a willow, adaptable as wind, yet steadfast as a diamond in your process.

〜〜〜〜〜〜〜〜〜

In Brief:

Honor your process.

Have fun!

Be gentle with yourself.

〜〜〜〜〜〜〜〜〜

Additionally,

- notice that there is creative use of capitalization and spelling. These are not typos. It has arrived this way on purpose to emphasize and identify inherent keys within written words. IT IS part of the Self's encoding available to you withinasthru your reading and experience of this handbook.

- consider, while reading this handbook, simultaneously discarding distractions as much as possible in terms of external things like TV, email, telephones, or other extraneous distractions. Make your time with IT a meditation, if you will.

- consider, as well, giving yourself permission to go a bit out of balance in moments. Sometimes you'll find that your most celebrated progress and life creations occur when you're completely out of balance.

- *practice until your practice becomes you.* Any practice done every day for a full moon cycle (28 days) becomes habit. And what you practice and how you practice becomes you. Ultimately, you reflect your habits as your life lived.

- use this handbook as you will. You can jump forward or simply ask a question, any question, then open IT up to help guide you to the answer already living within-nasthru you. Be playful with it and it will return the favor.

~~~~~~~~~~~~~~~~~~~~~~~~~~~~~~~~

Clarity Considerations

In addition to the considerations above, it is also important to introduce you to a few words, and their perhaps unique definitions, used throughout this handbook. There may be many meanings for the words used here. However, for the purposes of this handbook, the following words are hereby defined as follows:

WithInAsThru—The four separate words of *with, in, as* and *through* (shortened to *thru*) combined into one word. It forms a clearer illustration of the complete process by which LIFE occurs, in both expression and experience, withinasthru that part of LIFE that is you. This new form, WithInAsThru, more clearly expresses your connection to the one energy, one information, one intelligence that IS LIFE and the magnetic creation process by which you create your life and LIFE as you experience IT to BE WithInAsThru yoU!

This Inevitable Moment—Is an invitation to allow your seeing and listening to experience this moment as inevitable. Not that moment, THIS MOMENT. Yes, this one. This moment is inevitable, which means that there is nothing about this moment that is alterable. When you see this moment as inevitable you are willingness enough to be able to respond to any circumstance, situation or person being who you are. When you see this moment as inevitable, you may more easily choose to be the change you seek in any of your perceived tomorrows.

LIFE—IS another word for the many names and faces of God (Allah, Buddha, Krishna, Jah, Ra, Yahweh), where the two words are interchangeable. LIFE IS GOD IS LIFE.

One Energy—One Information–One Intelligence—Is an extended, more scientific expression for that which IS LIFE.

BEing—When BEing is written with the capital BE, it is an expression of the eternal IS, the All and the Everything, LIFE experiencing LIFE as the One Energy, the One Information, the One Intelligence that IT IS.

Being—Is the way by which you get to experience BEing as this part of LIFE that is you.

Self—Self is yet another way of saying BEing or LIFE. IT IS a word that invites enlightenment where the Seer, the Seen and the Scenery merge into one experience of this inevitable moment.

What IS—IS simply What IS, where the observed, observable and observer are seen, known, and experienced withinasthru this inevitable moment.

Self-Coding—A process by which you act upon your knowing that your life has no meaning save the meaning you give; and through this process you give purpose and meaning to your life, withinasthru your own I AM Poem, your poem as lived.

Ashea—And So IT IS

Welcome

Welcome

You remembered.
You arrived
To this inevitable moment.

Well Come.

Thank you
For your readiness.

Truth IS,
You've always been ready...

**Willingness Enough,
To Be Change,
Sought.**

Congratulations.

IT IS withinasthru sincere openness
And grateful humility
You have come
To now acknowledge and honor,
To choose and experience,
Who You Are.

Your every decision
To move forward,
Your purest choice,
Withinasthru courageous vulnerability,
To choose Self.

BE Cause.

Nothing in life happens to you.
Your life,
As you live IT,
Exactly as IT IS,
IS Occurring WithInAsThru yoU!

Breathe,

Smile,

Know,

Clear choice intention,

Ask grateful,

Giving,

Receptive.

Choose now
To live on purpose
LIFE as you choose IT to BE.

Choice IS.

Choose Well.

A. S. Kurslf

WithInAsThru
Open Consideration

This handbook has arrived as a result of your clearest intention for IT, as an experience to a request you have made.

Yes, you – your intention, your request and your willingness to receive IT.

Your willingness alone is cause for celebration, because you've been seeking for a very long time. You've asked for guidance and a companion to help illuminate the journey in front of you with the awareness of both knowing and unknowing.

Turns out, your humility in not knowing is the doorway for you to have become willingness enough. Well done.

You're here now as a result of your willingness to BE so.

In this inevitable moment, you are willingness enough to be receptive. And your willingness to receive is all that is ever asked of you in order to live LIFE, as you choose IT to BE, on purpose.

Yes, IT IS as simple as this. And yet even now you're being pulled by yesterday's beliefs to again complicate the process further.

Why? To what purpose?

By now, at least in glimpses, you've noticed the Presence withinas-thru this moment's inevitability. IT IS a river flowing deeper and wider to clear choice intentions, asked withinasthru gratitude, given away freely, willingness enough to receive it back, no matter form, on purpose, true.

This handbook is no different than the countless moments you've already called forth. Like that time you thought of just the perfect song, and a moment later you hear it playing in the next room on the radio; or just the other morning when you thought of your oldest friend, only to find an email from her when you next checked your inbox.

Coincidence is a term left to those who don't know or at least are still pretending they don't.

Smile.

Breathe deeply. And move forward withinasthru gratitude as you consider the following idea…

You are Source
Of every moment
You are.

This thought alone is enough. This thought is enough, once applied withinasthru gratitude, for you to be, do, and have your clearest desires fulfilled spontaneously, this inevitable moment you are.

All that is requested is your readiness and willingness to receive what you've asked for. Are you, then, willingness enough to consider…

Nothing in life happens to you,
Your life,
As you live IT,
Exactly as IT IS,
IS Occurring WithInAsThru you!

Live in your YES! You're ready. You've arrived in right and perfect timing, willingness enough to receive this handbook's truest offering…

To Live On Purpose,
LIFE as You Choose IT to BE.

The purpose of this handbook, as guide and journey companion, is to assist you in choosing again your power to be at cause in the matter of your life. The time has come, for at least a few of you, to begin again to see your world, your circumstances, your situations, your friends, your family, even your perceived enemies as a mirror reflection of you.

You are THAT you are.

No one and nothing IS separate from you. There is but one energy, one information, one intelligence that IS all of LIFE.

Separation is an illusion that no longer serves you or the greater good. Releasing the illusion of separation IS the core consideration offered here. To this end, this handbook is most clearly experienced Self to self.

Because there isn't anything you're about to read in the following pages that you don't already know. You're not here to find something to know. You're here to come consistently to the experience of knowing that you know withinasthru your unknowing, and to then act upon your knowingness to experience yourself as wisdom.

The journey you're embarking upon, page by page, will help you put your smile of knowingness into every one of your creations.

What is your smile of knowingness? It's a smile so full of gratitude for What IS, that gratitude itself has become your only true source of certainty.

So, by all means, ask gratefully, "Who would I BE? What would I DO? What would I HAVE? How would I live? What passions live deep inside me, ready to be fulfilled? To what purpose? Why?"

Consider again…

Nothing in life happens to you,
Your life,
As you live IT,
As you choose IT To BE,
Exactly as IT IS,
IS Occurring WithInAsThru you!

When you show up experiencing this moment's inevitability, you show up differently, don't you? You see and experience what is gratefully, perhaps even playfully. You make different decisions about who you are and who you choose to show up as. You're much more willing to live on purpose. Willingness enough to be the change you sought externally but a moment ago.

Be with this consideration for just a moment longer.

Take a deep breath. Smile. Know. Be grateful.

Gratitude, as your certainty, "to BE or not to BE?" This IS a question. Your life, exactly as IT IS, precisely as you Live IT, as you Choose IT to BE – your answer.

Or do you still believe it's possible to somehow be victim, without choice?

If you're adamant about being victim, you need not continue with this handbook at this time. Its gift you'll perceive to be impractical, unreal or even impossible.

Worry not. A moment from now, you'll find yourself once again in open consideration and humble Self inquiry.

Perhaps then you'll choose to cease pretending you're something that you're not, somehow separate from that which you desire.

So, if you're committed more to being a victim than living your life on passionate purpose, please be at least willingness enough to receive this final consideration for now.

A life lived on purpose and a life lived as victim are mutually exclusive paths. You cannot live on purpose and be victim in same moment. At some point along your journey, you'll be asked to choose.

Consider this handbook's arrival one such request, if you will.

However, if you're ready, willingness enough, to drop the chains of your self-imposed limitations, then you really are ready to be, do and experience life at full choice, and on purpose.

By all means, choose well.

Because throughout the evolution of humanity, **ALL have been called. Yet, very few of you have been willingness enough to choose Self.**

Will you choose Self?

Say YES!

And as a companion to your journey, this handbook is but an ever experienced reflection to this question:

What IS IT that's true for you?

It is suggested that you get clearer and clearer as to what is simply true for you, then act on What IS most true for you without hesitation. Boldness has genius, power and magic!

Be emboldened withinasthru humility to remain open, receptive, choosing, becoming. Withinasthru gratitude as your certainty, you will come to know that the puzzle of life you've been working on since birth is your puzzle, created by you to be solved withinasthru you, your life, lived.

No one else can solve or put together your puzzle for you. Only you can align the pieces so they form the image you imagine your Self to BE, expressed and experienced.

Perhaps these ideas seem impossible right now. Perhaps life has been hectic, discouraging, and filled with suffering, even misery. You may feel that it's all been falling apart, or that it's about to. And you've done everything you know to do, said everything you've known to say, asked every question you could possibly ask, and yet still you're ever seeking, ever wanting, ever needing something or someone. You may even hallucinate you've come here, to this handbook, to find that which you've sought all along.

Well come to this moment's reflection, Self to self.

Because you are every moment you are...

Well Come Back to Self!

Welcome back to the knowingness that always arrives when you're willingness enough to receive what you have asked for.

What you have been seeking IS yoU!

Consider this: Right when it appears that IT's all falling apart (your life, your relationships, your sense of control), IT's really all falling back together at the next highest level. Not merely better or different, but a complete transformation deep WithInAsThru yoU. Your choice to BE that which you've sought for so long in external ways.

It's you. Yes, yoU!

Imagine that your life is a mirror reflection of who you're being in relationship to LIFE. Your friends are a mirror reflection of who you're being in relationship to this part of you that IS your friends. The same is true in relationship to your entire life 360 degrees spherically.

It's you. IT's always been yoU!

You are the only constant in your life. You're the only one who's been present with you every moment you are. And it's time you stopped pretending it could ever be another's fault or that you could ever truly be a sufferer, separate somehow from that which IS LIFE.

The crutch of needless suffering, the lie of separation dies today. It is an uninspired wine that keeps you drunk in disempowerment, corrupting your ability withinasthru blame, complain, explain, attack and defense.

Its deceptive presence in your life has caused you to numb yourself with suffering and misery, drama and pain, illusions of control played to boredom, hallucinations of false power through force that have corrupted your experience of Self.

It is again important to know that nothing in this handbook is either true or false, right or wrong, serving or disserving, unless IT IS such an experience for you. Be absolutely clear about this. Agreed?

Lean not on the beliefs of others. What you experience as truth becomes your truth, both form and matter. Form as by that which you perceive LIFE. Matter as in what now exists in your life.

Your truth then IS what you experience withinasthru your whole body – physically, mentally, emotionally and spiritually.

When you feel something, really feel the experience, there's nothing anyone can do or say to convince you that what you experienced didn't happen. No one could persuade you that it didn't occur, can they?

Why is that?

Because what you experience as truth IS your truth.

Keep this in both heart and mind during the course of your journey here. What's true in this handbook is only true for you if you experience IT as truth. If you find yourself wanting to believe it true, let it go. It will not serve you. It must be truth to you, for you, withinasthru you completely for it to show up in your life as form and matter.

Consider beliefs to be sand traps on the course of your journey back to Self.

Trust your fullest and most expressive experiences. Your internal guidance never fails to bring you home.

Home IS your willingness to feel IT, whatever IT IS, completely.

Let go of any myth that you no longer experience as truth, as you will. Let your life, lived, become home to others seeking the same.

Give guidance and willingly be fellow journey companion as invited. Your way is no better than hers. Her way is no better than yours, no better than his.

Be completely clear that just like you, they too have always been the living answer to every question they've ever asked.

This is eternally so.

Consider further that you've been letting people tell you what to do with your life since birth. As result, you've been eager to do the same to others.

You've all been told who to be and why you're here, perhaps by well-meaning friends and family or by outdated belief systems that no longer serve you or the greater good. Because their roots live too deep within the illusion of separation, the beliefs of your more prominent cultural stories and religious dogmas may no longer serve you or the greater good. If they no longer serve you, be willingness enough to let them go.

Consider again that your outdated beliefs and cultural dogmas are making believe illusions to be true for survivability reasons, not as guideposts along the path of your, or humanity's, illumination.

If you've ever made believe you can be a victim, you too have been tightly wrapped in the blanket of separation. War and suffering in your time is a direct reflection.

It could safely be proposed, withinasthru the lens of history, that in the moments just before humanity's awakening, most were walking around expressing and participating in insanity.

Be, then, sane in a world of insanity.

Choose to be the change sought. Be and live responsibly, completely able and willing to be the change you seek.

You need not agree with what is, simply see what is as What IS, and choose to accept IT, as IS. Your choice to accept What IS causes quantum expansion in your ability to respond to this inevitable moment, Being as you choose to BE, Living as you Choose to Live.

Choose then to live on purpose.

Withinasthru your deeds, you are known.

Right here, right now, get quiet, be still. Know. Apply what you know. Be wise. Let go of all that is no longer serving you and the greater good, as you will. Stop pretending illusions of separation to be real. Choose to release all regrets, resentments, and grievances.

You're the miracle you've been waiting for.

Wait no more.

Ask yourself, "How's waiting been working for me?" Probably, waiting has you pretending your life is not going as well as you would perhaps tell others in transparent moments. Or worse, your life is becoming filled with more and more distractions designed to pull you ever faster into numbness, wanting more but feeling less and less. And somehow you're actually relieved by the numbness. You've come to depend on it. You hallucinate you need it.

You have actually set up your life with many distractions, all of which are designed to keep you from feeling any real emotions.

Is this really the life you desire? Is this really how you define success?

One final consideration TO BE asked of yoU, prior to completely engaging this handbook. And IT IS this:

Please consider that you're pretending it all up. All of IT. ALL that you experience as LIFE, your Life as IT IS.

Consider seeing IT this way:

> **Pre** – *what was before.*

> **Tend** – *what you pay attention to.*

The key to this shift is to pretend withinasthru your truth, experienced and felt to expressions complete, rather than the lies masquerading as borrowed beliefs or cultural dogmas.

It's time to script a new myth.

It's time to write a new poem.

It's time you wrote and sang your most authentic song, and danced as if the very marrow of your life depends upon IT. Because IT does.

It's time now to play this wonderful game of life as it was intended to be played.

LIFE IS not a game you can win.

LIFE IS not a game you can lose.

LIFE IS a game that can only be played.

IT's how you play the game – that IS, who you're Being in relationship to LIFE as IT IS - in this inevitable moment - that makes the difference between experiencing yourself as a magnificent co-creator or experiencing yourself as a sufferer to some other's cause and effect.

Be at Source and Cause to this inevitable moment you are.

As you are, IT IS.

You've come once more to the very beginning, where all possibilities come alive.

WithInAsThru this Living Consideration, enter this journey knowing each knows their parts agreed to long before.

Time, no time.

Space, no space.

Lifetimes beyond concept of lifetimes, you've arrived, this moment complete.

Self's contract IS to bring a living consideration, experienced and expressed as this handbook, as co-authored with you, the reader. Your contract, as reader, IS to read what has been co-authored here and to apply what IS true for you, into your living wisdom.

Let this journey then continue.

Again, welcome back to Self.

Ashea.

Clear

Choice

Intention

Ask

Grateful

Giving

Receptive

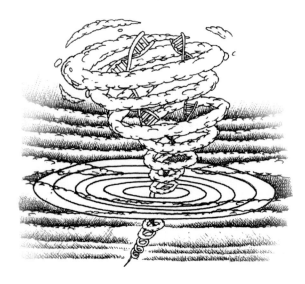

7 Processes to Live On Purpose

There are seven processes by which you will come to understand how your life, as you live IT, IS occurring WithInAsThru yoU. These seven processes are circular and spiral vertically as would a tornado. Meaning, their order is significant only by which door you choose to enter first. As you choose, so too do you reflect who you are in this inevitable moment, you are. Each Choice IS as perfect, whole and complete as you make IT.

For the purpose of this handbook, the processes will be offered in the order by which you will receive the largest benefit and the quickest result. Those of you who have already done a lot of work to get abundantly clear about who you are may simply find the first three processes a way to deepening wisdom.

The processes, in clearest order, live indelibly in this poem:

Clear Choice Intention
Ask Grateful
Giving
Receptive

Within each of these processes, you'll also find practices to experiment with. These are clear, direct ways to allow each process to become your practice. Each of these practices are offered as additional consideration for your experimentation on your journey to living LIFE as you choose IT to BE. Use them as you will.

Clear

Choice

Intention

Ask

Grateful

Giving

Receptive

Clear

What Does It Mean to BE Clear?

*I*magine a deer eating peacefully in a green, open field. It begins to saunter off, and then bounds freely across the meadow. The deer is clear. The deer lives integrally as deer. She is clear because she is congruent in form and function BEing deer.

Clearing is to become as congruent as nature. A lion is lion. A tree is tree. To be clear is a choice to so fully experience this moment's inevitability that this moment's inevitability becomes you—where seer, seen and scenery merge into the Self awareness that you are every moment you are.

It's a choice you make every day in relationship to the thoughts you think, the words you say, the stories you live with, who and what you surround yourself with, and the way in which you live your life.

Clearing, as a process, is a conscious act of releasing any and all perceived suffering on an ongoing basis. It's a conscious choice to heal any perceived past wounds, real or imaginary, that keep you trapped in infinite loops of relived suffering and misery. It's a choice to let go of all your reasons why not, being so harmonious in your YES! that you arrive into this moment's inevitability fully integrated and congruent withinasthru your complete body— your physical body, your emotional body, your mental body or Mind, and your spiritual body, also known as your energy body, or subtle body.

To be clear and integral is your natural way of Being.

Note to self...
> **BE Clear.**

A Practice to Clear
WithInAsThru Breath

3 Breaths to Clear that part of Self that is you...

*T*his habit is one you'll want to integrate fully. It's a practice designed to help you be clear. It's a practice you may choose to engage as you wake up each morning, to center yourself in times of stress, and to realign your desires to what most serves you and the greater good.

With each of these three breaths, close your eyes and really feel.

Your first breath is to remember to breathe. Remember to be the calm inside the tornado, rather than the chaos of the storm. Any time you're feeling off, engage this first breath to simply remember to breathe.

Breathing brings you immediately back into the centeredness of choice, rather than the craziness of reaction.

Close your eyes and take this first breath now—the breath to remember to breathe.

The second breath is to remember to smile. Smile as you inhale, and extend your smile throughout your face as you exhale. This smile is to anchor into your facial muscles' memory your smile of knowingness. Again, this is your smile so full of gratitude that gratitude lives now as your truest source of certainty.

Regardless of situations or circumstances, you can always choose to smile. It is a choice only you can make. Because no matter what it is, all the good or the bad, no matter ecstasy or joy or how much pain or suffering you're in—this too shall pass. No matter what IT IS—this too shall pass. Because IT always does.

Close your eyes, light your face with your knowingness smile, and breathe your second breath—the breath to remember to smile.

The third breath is to remember to feel gratitude. By this point, most of the endorphins have returned you to more presence withinasthru this inevitable moment. Find your own way of deeply feeling gratitude as your certainty. Your choice here is to more fully engage the smile of knowingness by tilting your head as if you're looking up to BEing to say,

"Thank you for bringing me
Into this inevitable moment,
Into this time and into this space,
Fully able to respond to this moment's occurrence.
I accept What IS,
Willingness enough to be change sought,
Gratitude Be my Certainty.
Ashea.
And so IT IS!"

You don't need a specific reason to feel grateful, though if you choose to focus on one, that's helpful as well. The intention of this breath's prayer is to feel deep gratitude for what is—being grateful for your breath, grateful for BEing itSelf.

The third breath is instilling the practice of gratitude.

Now, with this third breath, as you're inhaling, look up, still smiling and really allow yourself to FEEL grateful and breathe your third breath—the breath to feel gratitude.

This simple practice of breathing—and it's one you can use as many times a day as you feel is helpful—works rapidly in terms of shifting the way that you attract life as you imagine it to be, in a way that serves you, serves those who you love and who love you, and serves a greater good.

As a quick review:
The first breath is to remember to breathe.

The second breath is to remember to smile.

The third breath is to remember to look up and feel gratitude for what is, right here, right now in this inevitable moment.

When life gets crazy or things get bent out of shape, remember to just simply breathe, smile, and be grateful for What IS.

This practice serves to remind you that you're always at choice in the process of creating life as you choose it to be. And it's a moment-to-moment choice you get to make.

May this moment's choice follow your clearest breath;
May your smile of knowingness be present
in this moment's decision;
And may gratitude be your certainty along your way.

Note to self...

Please, remember to breathe, especially in those moments you feel off. It'll help.

I Promise.

Why IS Being Clear Integral?

"Confidence without Clarity is dangerous."
—Sadhguru

The clearer you become, the less you choose to suffer What IS this moment's inevitability. The key to living LIFE as you Choose IT to BE isn't something you'll ever find outside of Self. The key arrives precisely in hand, in the exact moment its presence is desired, the moment you stop pretending what isn't true.

What's true is that what you desire and the key to make it so is you. IT couldn't be any other way. It is, however, very possible to live illusions true. You can very easily create experiences by which neither your desire nor the key to your desires is discovered. You may already know this ineffective way of living, intimately.

You can be certain there is more clearing to do as long as you are alive. Your work is to become as clear a receptor as you will. More specifically, in any moment you show up blaming, complaining, explaining, justifying, attacking or defending, you can be certain there is a misperception alive withinasthru you that would serve you most to release and let go. Any practice or habit that includes these disempowered states of being ensure an experience of humility is but a moment away.

When you clear yourself, you let go of the emotional baggage that keeps you stuck, that keeps you from fulfilling your greatest dreams, embodying your deepest desires. It's a process, yes, and not always the easiest of processes to apply into living wisdom. But when you make the initial choice to clear, to let go of your emotional pain-body and allow what IS to occur inevitably as

What IS, you open up a whole new world of beautiful possibilities you couldn't have even dreamed of a moment before.

> *"I feel it now... there's a power in me to grasp*
> *and give shape to my world. I know that nothing*
> *has ever been real without my beholding it."*
> —*Rainer Maria Rilke*

Note to self...
                        Be Clear. Be Cause.

The Emotional Pain-Body

The emotional pain-body is as real and as present in you as your physical body in terms of energy, information, and intelligence. However, because you don't see it with your eyes, you have spent little time considering its presence or questioning its purpose.

A very illustrative presentation is introduced by Eckhart Tolle in his best-selling book *The Power of Now*. While you'll learn a little about the emotional pain-body here in this handbook, please refer to his incredible book for more information if you desire a greater depth of understanding your emotional pain-body.

Briefly, the emotional pain-body is the wounded you, the wounded little boy you, the wounded little girl you, that, real or imagined, perceives an experience of suffering that has left its imprint upon your entire perceptual field. While it lives withinasthru your emotional body, the emotional pain-body, when activated, brings to life the wounded you into full 360-degree life experience.

When the emotional pain-body is activated, others might perceive you as someone other than you, definitely "not" yourself. Perhaps you've seen it rear its head when you've had a disagreement with your spouse. It may even be possible that your emotional pain-body takes over quite suddenly. When you're tired and depleted from a hard day, and you yell or act or speak violence in such a way that would be otherwise inconceivable to you, it's likely that your pain-body has been activated.

Regardless of the ways and means by which it arrives—and there are much more sinister and twisted forms of its presence available in your cultural news and stories—it's a shadow, sometimes a very deep, dark shadow; and it filters reality through a lens of continued suffering as you would perceive and thus experience it.

It's one of the true barriers to being happy. And when, as an exposed wound, it lives with you day after day in its various forms—from guilt and shame to fear and anger—your life takes on the attributes living withinasthru your emotional pain-body. It can be very challenging to break its cycle and patterns of experience, especially when you are immersed in its dramas of suffering.

It will keep you trapped eternally in yesterdays, pouring lemon juice and salt on the wounds you have been unable to heal completely. It keeps you forever alive with the possibility of suffering as your way; when in truth, no such suffering need exist.

Your emotional pain-body, no doubt, has been the greatest barrier to your desire to live on purpose. So how do you deal with this shadow entity that resides deeply withinasthru your emotional body?

Awareness alone is 90% of any transformation if you so trust and allow. Be aware of your patterns and your reactions. Observe yourself more and more without judging yourself. When you notice yourself being blame or complain, observe the observable and simply ask yourself, "Does this way of being serve me or my purpose?" The answer, as inevitable as this moment, will guide you to rapidly choose to complete whatever the perceived feeling of suffering.

Pain, unlike suffering, helps you become aware of where your emotional pain-body is still alive and kicking within you. Therefore, BE with your feelings. Feel the pain. That which you truly allow yourself to feel, you can complete. You can heal it and be clear once again. It's a choice you get to make often, day-to-day, moment-to-moment. Awareness alone can help you along this process.

As you begin to practice observing who you show up as, you'll bring the light of awareness to the shadows of your emotional pain-body. Be this awareness often enough and you'll clearly recognize that you're at complete choice as to whether your pain continues to direct you, or you it. Choose to heal your emotional pain-body and its many destructive attributes, and your problems will transform into extraordinary opportunities to be and live more clearly.

Additionally, the most direct way to feel the guidance of your emotional pain-body is withinasthru a practice of daily silence. To engage in this practice is to allow this inevitable moment to flow withinasthru you, as unfiltered and as unobstructed as you are willing and able. As this practice becomes you, you'll be clear and unhindered to live life, as you choose it to be, on purpose.

As you are and live, so too do you become a living possibility for humanity to also be and live.

Note to self...
Live clear. Choose to practice Self awareness.
Choose a practice of being silence, daily.

The Ecstasy of Self Silence

"All of man's miseries derive from his not being able to sit quietly in a room alone and enjoy the company he keeps."

—Pascal

That which is known is the only true limitation. It's in the unknown where all possibilities exist. Therefore, spend time each day in silence. Learn to enjoy the innerverse as much as you do the outer one.

Moments experienced withinsthru silence are a form of meditation. Yet there's a grander possibility inherent in silence. Being silence brings you back into the experience of the nothingness by which you come. The gap between thoughts is the seam into existence itself, just as the silence in between the music notes holds the song in sweet perfection. Yet even as the deepest nothingness of your innerverse comes to mirror the nothingness of the farthest reaches of space, there you are observing.

Be at one with the exhale of existence, something from something, as you are with the inhale of existence, you from nothingness. Let your inhale come into balance with your exhale. As your breath becomes one with the all and the everything, you'll come to know breath as the doorway by which you travel from nothingness into who you are this inevitable moment you are.

Your breath will guide you into coherence, as you come to receive the gift silence brings you. Being silence is a gift of unspeakable proportions, allowing you the experience, even if just glimpses, of experiencing the vastness you really are. Consider this simple experiment:

Picture yourself, right now, from just above where you are sitting. Look at the top of your head, the couch or bed or chair you're sitting in, experience you looking at you from above. Now move your consciousness out, and picture the building you're in from outside and above it. Move further out and see the town you live in as if you're in a helicopter. See it in perspective of the entire landscape of the countryside. Now go out even further and see the earth as an astronaut would see it—blue oceans mixed with the greens and browns of earth, beneath the swirls of white clouds. Now go even further—let earth become a dot, illuminated in the vastness of space. See now the sun become but a distant star, earth a long-ago memory.

Incredible? Beautiful? Yes. But nothing more than you are. Become Self aware. Who is it that's seeing and observing? No matter how far out you go, is it not still you? Are you not still present as seer and observer? Yes, you are.

Now bring it all the way back and go inside. Be aware that no matter how far you go inside to the very space in between your cells, the eternal dance of energy and information right down to the quarks and bosons, there you are. Even as you move through timeless time and spaceless space, you are every moment you are. A seer that is timeless, you are the ever-present observer, connected to this inevitable moment, eternally. And eternally this is so.

What being silence gives you, then, is the understanding that no matter how deep you go inside, or how far you explore the outer realm, you ARE. And you are that you are. This understanding helps free you of the emotional pain-body. It helps to clear all unnecessary and needless suffering, because it gives you a glimpse of the vastness you are, making the wounds you carry less potent and entirely less real.

Consider the ecstasy of silence a living practice of BEing withinasthru silence. It's a very real practice by which you clear. The more time you spend in silence, the clearer you become. It's a fantastic gift, because you really come to experience that you're none of the things you thought you were. You're so much more. And then the knowingness of being so much more allows you the Self awareness to heal yesterday's perceived wounds and misperceptions.

Note to self...

Be still and know that you are a no body. When you become okay with being a no body, only then will you truly allow yourself to be a somebody with purpose.

A Practice to BE Silence

A practice of daily silence allows you to use the innerverse to help you clear any of yesterday's sufferings, while concurrently giving you access to infinite intelligence.

Therefore, make daily mediation, daily silence, a practice. Practice daily silence until it becomes habit. Reap the benefits and the rewards that can only come from within your innververse.

While there are many different types and practices of meditation you can engage in, consider this simple practice.

Set aside about 10 minutes daily to begin a practice. This is all you'll need to create tangible experiences withinasthru the gift of silence. Now, find a comfortable position to sit in, or lay in, if that's your preference. Make sure all distractions are turned off and tuned out—you'll want as little extraneous noise as possible.

Close your eyes and breathe deeply, concentrating on the spot just between your eyes. Now, take a deep breath, feel it as deeply as you possibly can, and hold the breath in your diaphragm for a count of three. Now exhale slowly. Breathe in this way for five breaths, inhaling through your nose and exhaling out your mouth. Let your inhale expand your diaphragm. Your exhale will contract it. As you breathe, concentrate on the way your diaphragm feels expanding and contracting. Feel the air as it enters your lungs and expands into your chest and belly. Be present to each inhale and exhale. Let your breathing find its own natural rhythm.

Remain in silence. Allow your mind to drift to and fro, from something into nothingness, back and forth. Do not pass judgment upon the thoughts that arrive. Simply observe them and let them float away. Feel your consciousness shift from the point between your eyes down your spine as you feel your whole body more integrally with each breath.

Become nothing, and in the nothingness, you'll start to experience the everything. As you desire, open your eyes and take a moment to realign yourself with the conscious world.

Try doing this exercise at least once a day for the next week—or until you find a practice that suits your personal preferences. As you grow accustomed to the silence, you'll be able to extend your meditation period for longer times, each time finding more ecstasy in the practice of silence.

Additionally, there are many meditation practices available, and even more teachers willing to instruct you and guide you into your own practice. Some practices are simple, while others are more complex. The right and perfect practice for you is the one that works and gets you the results you seek.

A resource center has been developed for this handbook online at *http://www.WithInAsThru.com/thehandbook/resources.*

There, you will find links designed to inform you and to steward you into finding the right practice for you.

Please use this resource center as you will. It has been designed to serve you in your choice to live on purpose, your life as you choose it to be.

> "A meditator is hooked to an EEG... the EEG machine shows an unmistakably novel series of brain wave patterns... the meditator is having experiences for which the word 'spiritual' seems most fitting: She is experiencing a sense of expanded consciousness, an increase in love and compassion, a feeling of encountering the sacred and numinous in both herself and the world at large."
> —Ken Wilber, "A Theory of Everything"

Note to self...
Practice being silence. It'll help more than you could imagine.

"I Am THAT I Am"

*"If I am walking with two other men,
each of them will serve as my teacher. I will
pick out the good points of the one and imitate
them, and the bad points of the other and cor-
rect them in myself."*

—Confucius

T hus, has the great I AM been offered throughout time as a way and a life. What does it mean for you when you say, "I Am That I Am?" Go ahead. Say it out loud, right now. "I Am That I Am." Now say it again, only this time with more emotion, "I Am That I Am!" Say it again, "I Am That I Am."

Now say it quietly to yourself as you look out the window. Look upon the swayfulness of the trees and say, "I Am That I Am." Look at the buildings, the cars, the people passing by. "I Am That I Am." Say it quietly to yourself as you go out to the grocery store or to the movies, "I Am That I Am." Let the words permeate your seeing, your listening, your very being, "I AM THAT I AM." Get that it doesn't matter what the "that" is, or who, because you are THAT you are.

That's IT. IT IS this simple. No matter where you go today, no matter where you are, no matter what you see, no matter who you see or see it with, no matter the scenarios, the people, the events, the situations, the circumstances… You Are THAT You Are.

You are every moment you are. You are THAT you are. Please allow this inevitable moment to wrap you in the stillness and the movement of who you really are. Choose to become IT.

Would you be willingness enough to consider, just for a mo-ment, trying on this expanded language? The next time you find yourself angry at another, simply consider that he is simply that part of you that is him. All that you judge in another, lives in you, or it couldn't exist in any moment you are. And you are every moment you are. Everything you've been seeing withinasthru him or her, in purest form, is a reflection of you.

You are THAT you are. The irony is that your judgment is a request from your Self to yourself to change, to release a pattern in you, to heal, to forgive. If you know that you're complete with that aspect of self that you would judge, then you're ready for another version of you. You're ready for another possibility, another experience, your next expression.

What more could you possibly be waiting for to take action, to move, to let the wind of your desires blow you in the direction of your dreams? Use judgments as discernments to call you ever more rapidly into being the change you desire to see in the world. Because no matter what you would be judging, it's you.

No matter what or who the "that" is, you are THAT you are—one energy, one information, one intelligence, you are that you are.

Note to self...

You are THAT you are.

Yes, Especially THAT!

The most painful judgments you hold are the hardest to see in the reflective mirror. You may ask, "How is what's written here possible? I'm not him or her. I'm not those people! I'm not the mess that is this world!"

It may be very difficult to initially receive this consideration as truth because you see so much anger, hatred, and violence in the world. And you aren't yet able to transcend the myths of separation so ingrained into your collective consciousness and social dogmas. This myth of separation is deeply rooted in your subconscious, making it very difficult in moments to see the inter-connectedness of LIFE. This myth lives in your social structures. It lives in your religious dogmas. Its roots are deep; its entrain-ment all but complete.

> *"The great enemy of the truth is very often not the lie, deliberate, contrived, and dishonest, but the myth: persistent, persuasive and realistic."*
> —John F. Kennedy

So, as you begin to apply the consideration, "You Are THAT You Are," to your life, you may experience a predictable amount of resistance and catharsis withinasthru your process of living. However, as you do, you'll continue to expand your awareness, becoming ever clearer that everything in life—LIFE itself—is but one energy, one information, and one intelligence.

This way of seeing life will become your way of seeing. And as you begin to let go of your own anger, hatred, and violence, you'll begin to see and encounter much less in your daily life, much less in the life you perceive and experience.

The more of you who choose this way of seeing, the more this way of seeing becomes life as experienced in your time.

Consider this for a moment. Imagine, if you would, an eternal en-ergy connection between you and all that you see. See this energy connection as an infinity symbol. Follow the infinity sign from your heart to whatever "that" you may be holding as separate—maybe it's your boss or spouse or perhaps the man on a street picking through the trash.

Just follow the opening curve of infinity's path to land on whatever "that" is present to you in this inevitable moment. Now allow its return, bending withinasthru the "that" back to your heart, completing the infinity sign. Now say aloud, "I am THAT I am," with an emphasis on the THAT.

Have fun with this. This alone can heal you forever. Get through your entire day completely comfortable with whatever "that" that shows up. And get, truly GET, you are THAT you are.

It's humbling, yet empowering, to see withinasthru Self awareness and clarity that you are THAT you are. You'll become very grounded withinasthru your willingness to let go of self-importance and self-judgment as you come to see and know the interconnectedness of every one and everything. The illusion of separation will again fade back into the nothingness from which it all comes. And you'll begin to feel the quickening of enlightenment as you come more and more to see withinasthru humility, "Oh yes, this too... I Am THAT I AM."

The next panhandler who comes upon your path, you'll know "I am that I am." And you'll be surprised to find that the completion to this thought is, "Thank you for BEing." Because you will no longer be able to see just a panhandler or a beggar, you will see and know only that part of Self that is beggar. From this point, you can heal the part of you that is beggar in any form by which you show up as beggar. You'll show up more and more able to respond loving your neighbor as yourself, because there is none other than Self.

Then, if you're so moved, you can give freely to him, as you would Self—attention, money, listening. Whatever the inevitability of this moment may request from you, you'll be able and willing to respond within your capability. You'll do what you are capable of doing to help heal his part of you that is beggar withinasthru true compassion and empathy.

As such, your humility will continue to bring you ever closer to the truer nature of life. Humility allows you to realize, "Oh, wow. I am that." A moment before, you may have been judging or attacking another, but now you see and know you were merely judging or attacking Self.

There's an expression that is commonly used today, "There but by the Grace of God go I." This practice of applying the "I Am THAT I Am" to your seeing will ask you to shift this statement to a new understanding: "There, WithInAsThru the Grace of BEIng, I Am."

"There is nothing that is known that's not knowable.
All that ever was, so too, were you.
All that is now, so too are you.
All that shall be, so shall you be
One energy. One information. One intelligence.
LIFE as IT IS."

Note to self...
  It's always the most challenging reflections to accept that bring the greatest transformation once seen as Self...
  Because even that, You are THAT you are.

What IS, IS What IS

"A man should look for what is,
and not for what he thinks should be."

Albert Einstein

Y ou have probably already arrived on your own to more effortlessly and joyfully perceive and experience What IS this inevitable moment. However, if you were to ask yourself, "Am I able to see What IS without coloring it with my desires, disappointments, unspoken expectations, denials, and lies?" Probably, you would not. At least, not yet. And that's okay, because the entrainment of this open consideration is already helping to expand and stabilize Self Awareness.

The Is, IS. It's what's occurring right here, right now. It's this inevitable moment. What does it mean to see this moment's inevitability?

Consider this moment. Not that one, this moment. Yes, this one.

This moment is inevitable, isn't it? Is there anything about this moment that can be altered? Now—not a moment from now—is there anything about this moment that is anything other than sure to occur? This moment's inevitability is just that—your willingness to see IT, exactly as IT IS, certain that IT is unalterable.

That's IT. That's all there IS to IT. This moment is inevitable exactly as IT IS. What IS is the actual event, circumstance, or situation—not the meaning projected upon it as good or bad, right or wrong—but the actual occurrence.

What IS is observable. It's what's so. The act of seeing What IS is the act of observing the observable, without opinion, without judgment, and without any possibility that this moment is anything other than inevitable.

> "Seek not the truth, merely withhold opinion."
> —Taoist saying

Practice this way of seeing What Is and you'll become instantly clearer in your ability to witness this inevitable moment.

Consider a situation where you've encountered something that might have been displeasing; for example, a mother yelling at her child in the supermarket. On one level, you're irritated with the mother, and you project what you think she should or should not be doing. But look deeper—look at the situation as it IS, not as you would want it to be.

> "Out beyond right doing and wrong doing,
> There is a field. I will meet you there."
>
> —*Rumi*

Notice the noise in your observation when you filter listening and seeing through yesterday's ideas of what is right and wrong. Instead, simply observe the observable. Observe IT as IT IS, not as you would wish it to be, and you'll become instantly clear on where your projections may be clouding a reality that was, a moment before, beyond your perception.

Now apply this to every encounter, every moment of your life. Stand aside from all you think you know to observe the IS as What IS, rather than what you wish it would be or could be or should be.

From this vantage point, you're coming ever more rapidly to bringing your whole Self into alignment again—physically, emotionally, mentally, and energetically. Withinasthru the coherence in your ability to see what is as What IS, you'll arrive into this inevitable moment fully willing and able to be responsible; that is, able to respond with authentic power, as requested.

Only withinasthru your responsibility will you be able to help respond to both woman and child in the most helpful of ways.

Note to self...

See What IS as What IS. Allow this moment's inevitability to become you. AND release forever any needless suffering and misery.

All Suffering Occurs WithInAsThru Your Resistance to What IS

All of your suffering and misery, All of IT, exists withinasthru your resistance to What IS. Such resistance doesn't allow you to experience this moment's inevitability. You're constantly seeking what's wrong or what needs to be improved. You're consistently saying "no" to what is, living forever in yesterday or tomorrow.

It is your resistance to What IS that keeps you in dead-end jobs with little to no fulfillment. It's your resistance to What IS that keeps you in unhealthy or abusive relationships without hope of a brighter tomorrow. It's your resistance to What IS that keeps you running from one numbing task or distraction to the next—wishing, hoping that somehow the number you get, the better you'll feel.

Sadly, you never feel better numbing yourself, because the more numb you are, the less you're able to feel. More likely, the number you get, the more you'll resist What IS. Eventually you'll choose to see what's missing or lacking, not what's present and complete. You'll choose to see what's wrong or misplaced, not what's perfect and whole.

As you see What IS, so too do you see Self.

Resistance has given you what you asked for. Because every time you've resisted What IS, at some level you were seeking to experience suffering of some kind. When you resist what is, you end up perpetuating the myth of separation. And that gives you permission to build walls thick, high, and wide to protect you from the remembrance, "You are THAT you are." Protective walls can be invaluable to you, if you truly believe you are your preconceived identity, or if you truly desire to keep alive the illusion of separation.

However, a wall can only keep out what you falsely believe you're not. Eventually, your beliefs of separation become your prison cell, bending your entire perceptual field to make believe that you really are just an identity, an identity that needs protecting and defense.

And so the spiral of your creation, LIFE as you're choosing to live it, becomes your IS. You'll justify IT as it's occurring. You'll rationalize IT. You'll even come to defend IT and attack others for seeing and experiencing IT differently than you do.

No war has ever been fought without each leader first declaring their need and right to defend their way of life, their IS.

You can rectify this, in this inevitable moment, by tossing resistance to the wind. Feel the flip-switch within your being every time resistance rears its head. Embrace the IS with a smile and a quick observation. See what IS as the Pre-Sent moment, sent to you, by yoU, for your own clearest experience of who you're being.

This is not to say that your seeing of what IS isn't valid, especially if pain and suffering have been a large part of your life story. Simply consider that the more you hold on to the way of suffering, the more suffering and misery exists withinasthru LIFE as you experience IT.

When you're not able to let go of your suffering and misery, when you're unable to see what is and dwell solely on your suffered version of what is, the pain and suffering will find a way to manifest in the very matter of your life—whether it's financial, a dysfunctional relationship, and even your body.

At root cause, all disease, that is dis-ease, exists as a result of your resistance to what is. Louise L. Hay wrote an incredible book called *You Can Heal Your Life*. Her basic message is that if you embrace life as it is, you can heal yourself. She healed herself from cancer. Imagine what you might be able to prevent when you choose to release your resistance to what is and choose to gratefully see What IS this inevitable moment.

*get busy living
or get busy dying,
victim no more
to whims of cultural dogma,
willingness enough
to play full out,
jumping into the river,
seeing and knowing,
you are THAT you are,
this inevitable moment
IS
What IS.*

How to Remain Clear

Breathe, smile and be grateful for this inevitable moment. Remain flexible and adaptable in your seeing and listening of others withinasthru your willingness to see and know, "You Are THAT You Are." Shatter the illusion of separation as a daily practice in the ecstasy of silence, returning again to the nothingness from which you come. Learn to love the company you keep in those silent moments alone. Resist no longer What IS. Accept what is as What IS to live fully able to respond to this inevitable moment.

LIFE IS much more fun and filled with much more joy than perhaps you've been willing to allow IT to Be. Allow LIFE to be fun and joy filled.

Note to self...

Be clear that you are always
at choice to be clear.

Clear?

Clear
Choice
Intention

Ask

Grateful

Giving

Receptive

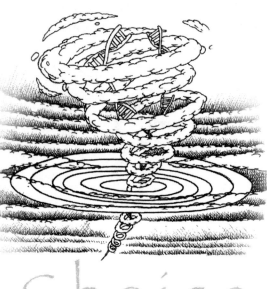

Choice

What does IT mean to BE at Choice?

Who you are Being IS a choice, right now, in this inevitable moment. IT IS a choice "to be or not to be". Shakespeare offered IT perfectly for your consideration. For "to be or not to be" is the question your life, exactly as it is, is answer to.

Who are you here to be and become? Get clear. Select. Choose. Decide. What is the path of purpose you're willing to choose? What does your passion tell you? What does your heart tell you? What is it you desire to be and do in your life? How do you wish to express yourself? What's calling you? Who are you choosing to be right now?

There was a 9-year-old boy named Thomas who was introduced withinasthru James Twyman's The Beloved Community. He gave a wonderful gift of guidance in an email where he shared, "… you've simply forgotten that you're pretending it all up."

Pre is what was before. Tend is what you pay attention to. And you're pretending it up, based on lies of separation, lies of disunity, and lies that you can be separate from God and separate from LIFE and separate from one another. It is time to pretend such lies into existence no more. Instead, choose to pretend it all up based on the truth of unity and oneness.

Once you choose to let go of these myths of separation, all of the hardships humanity faces today—poverty, hunger, war, suffering of any kind—will disappear over night. Because you'll be pretending IT up based on what's true, you will create heaven on earth with effortless joy and ease.

However, you get to choose now who you are and why you're here. Never doubt again that you're always at choice to be who you desire to be and live as you desire to live. Yet, until you actively ask the question "Who am I?" you'll be living without a horizon to steer your purpose upon, you'll be pretending that you're somehow not always at choice in who you are being.

And you are eternally at choice.

As you consistently ask yourself who you are, you'll move to the next level of courageous vulnerability that begins to additionally ask, "Why not by my design and on my terms? Why not live a life that not only I dream about, but a life worthy of me? Why not travel a path, certain withinasthru my gratitude for What IS, leaving the road behind me illuminated so that others may easily follow? Why not?"

If you're ready to ask such bold questions with the awareness that you're completely and eternally at choice as to every specific detail you are and will ever be, then you are clear here.

> Note to self...
> You are always at choice.
> Choose well.

Why IS BEing at Choice Integral?

*B*eing at choice, consciously, allows you to observe what IS—able to choose and respond to this inevitable moment exactly as who you choose to be. Now, this won't entitle you to falsely control another's actions or feelings. Such control is an illusion. Seek it no further. However, you are always at choice in your response to another's actions and feelings. As you choose, so too do you create your life as you choose it to be. Because ultimately your life, precisely as it is, is a sum total of every choice you've ever made.

As an example, in a moment of heated argument with a spouse, you find yourself wanting to lash out. Being at choice, however, gives you the opportunity to take a breath, step back, observe the situation, and make your next decision based on the answer to this question, "Who am I here to be?" You've learned to observe the observable, without judgment, and you're able to choose wisely based on your stated desires.

Be this awareness in relationship to the people and circumstances of your life. Being at choice in this inevitable moment moves you concurrently to Being clear.

Note to self...
> You're always at choice!
> Again, choose well.

How to Remain Ever at Choice

"No problem can be solved from the same level of consciousness that created it."
—*Albert Einstein*

Awareness is 90% of your process in being and becoming the solution to any problem you now face. How freeing is that? Being aware of any of your perceived troubles is 90% of the journey to letting them go, to healing them, to elevating your level of consciousness, and to becoming the solution to them. That you're aware means you're already on course. Please know that you wouldn't be here right now, reading this handbook, if you weren't ready on various levels to become the changes you seek in your life.

Wherever there's a pattern in your life, there's a choice. As you get clearer and clearer with the pattern, your choices begin to reveal themselves to you. Your work is to choose a new pattern that serves you and the greater good.

Perhaps you have a pattern of watching television for hours every night. It's possible you're semi-depressed and have a hard time playing with your children. This way of being has probably become a pattern in your life. Be ever aware of your patterns. Where there's a pattern, there's a choice. You have this power of choice. Accept this power to choose and act upon your choice. Regardless of your reasons, you are at choice. If you're depressed, get angry. If you're angry, get courageous. Wherever you're at, choose a new feeling that will elevate you and your life's condition.

Here's the incredible news—simply by choosing a new feeling, you can allow your choices to flow more freely. Because it's okay to feel. It's more than okay, it's imperative. If you feel depressed, that's okay. When you're tired of being depressed, choose another way of feeling. Start getting angry, or courageous, or happy— anything to jar you out of your pattern of depression and into a space where choice and change again flows more freely.

It takes great courage, courageous vulnerability, to get to a point where you're ready to be the change, a change that, a moment ago, you were seeking in the "outside" world. Once you're clear change is possible, you're at choice.

Choose.

It really is this simple.

Choose with consistency as your choices become you. When you slip back into an old, tired pattern, release the judge and the critic. Observe that you're in a pattern, a pattern that you are completely at choice withinasthru. Then, choose the pattern that more closely matches where you are now or where you desire to be instead of where you were a moment ago.

How can you shift the pattern permanently? Jump into the experience of your new choice. Keep jumping into the experience, whether it's playing with your children, eating less at every meal, or making more money with effortless joy and ease. Whatever the new choice is, immediately, right now, in this inevitable moment, choose to jump into experience.

Nothing transforms you quicker than experience because once you've experienced your self as this new choice, you've become it. This is who you are. You're now being who you but dreamt of being only a moment ago. And you're being so experientially.

> Note to self...
>
> Your dreams come to life withinasthru
> your willingness to choose them.
>
> Because you're always at choice,
> by all means choose them.

Creatively Choose Life
WithInAsThru Desire

Life is not a process of discovery, but a process of creative choice. As you choose to consciously engage the process of creative choice, the first step is getting to clarity about what it is you desire. Desire is the beginning to creating your dreams true. Desire is first thought. It is a heart passion felt within your very being.

Withinasthru desire comes the eternal remembrance… "Ask and IT shall be given. Knock and the door shall be opened." Desire is your way of asking, your process of knocking. The promise IS that you always get what you ask for. The opportunity is to become clearer and clearer withinasthru your process of asking. Perhaps this is why you've arrived here, now to this inevitable moment.

Because once you have clarity of desire, you'll choose to engage the process further with your very next thought. Thought energy is the opening rung through the doorway of creative choice. Your every experience first arrives withinasthru thought—that idea that arrives while showering, the concept that brings one of the "ah ha" moments on a project you've been working on, or the vision that you awake with in the middle of the night. Everything—everything—was once but someone's idea, an idea they chose to create out of infinite possibilities. Nothing exists, or lives in existence, that did not first exist as pure thought!

> *"Think left and think right and think low and think high. Oh, the things you can think up if only you try!"*
> —Dr. Seuss, *"Oh, The Thinks You Can Think!"*

Thought is the initial spiral of creative choice. Next is word. Words are thoughts expressed. Word is creative and sends forth creative energy withinasthru your life lived. Words are more vibrant than thought, because words occur differently withinasthru you once spoken. With greater impact, they disrupt or change the field of creation as you've engaged IT.

Words are the secondary spiral of creative choice.

Action follows.

Engage fully in the process of creative choice because your life IS as you choose IT to BE. Even as you read these words, your life IS occurring withinasthru you. This is your power. This is the magnetic creator you are. This is the truth of your promised ability to ask and receive whatever IT IS you desire.

All that you see or is seeable in your world is the outcome of your idea about IT. Again, this is because life is a process of creative choice, not discovery. Live each day not to discover what it holds for you, but to create it, to choose it, to receive IT. You are, in no uncertain terms, creating your reality withinasthru this inevitable moment.

You wouldn't have come. You wouldn't have been looking. You wouldn't have done a Google search. You wouldn't have clicked on an ad. You wouldn't have been searching online in the middle of God knows what hour surfing or strolling upon the book store aisle for another doorway, searching for a new way, if you weren't ready to receive IT.

Receive IT withinasthru Gratitude. Let gratitude be your certainty.

Know that you are completely at choice. Let your passions show the way. Allow your desires to lead you deeper through the doorway opened by your gratitude of What IS.

Focus. Think about what you desire to BE. Think about what kind of things you'd be doing if you were being who you desire to be. What else would you do? What would you have? Think about your desires often. Live with them. Sleep with them. Dream about them.

Imagine no other possibilities. Expand what is possible. Embody gratitude as your certainty. Release all doubts. Jump into the river of experience of your new choices lived. Discipline your mind.

And get supremely committed to the original creative thought that initially moved, touched and inspired you to choose IT.

Because when your thoughts are clear and steadfast as diamonds, you'll begin to speak them as truths withinasthru gratitude, appreciating possibilities into probabilities as a result of your certainty.

Certain, you'll begin to say them out loud. Using the great command "I AM," you'll come to speak them withinasthru the integral creative power you are.

"I AM" is the strongest creative statement in the universe. Whatever you think and say after the words "I AM" sets into motion the very experiences requested. It calls the great universal IS to your aide, magnetically attracting to you the life of your dreams, lived withinasthru full expression and gratitude complete.

Now act.

And so IT IS.

> Note to self...
>
> Let your desires lead you towards
> living a life of your dreams.
>
> Allow the great "I AM" to steward
> your very becomingness.

Now,
allow awareness to enter,
allowing,
means you're on course,
a promise,
made from Self,
to self,
willingness enough,
to become the change,
you've sought,
in others,
the world,
as IS,
changes in mirror,
reflection,
you,
as source.

The Power of a Neutral Mind

Never underestimate the power of a neutral mind and a neutral heart.

In a society filled with condemnations and judgments, and demands from all sides regarding what's right and what's wrong, neutrality may seem contrary to all you've been taught. But allowing yourself the gift of neutrality is an inherent step to conscious evolution.

So what is neutrality? It's being able to observe the observable without forming an opinion of right or wrong. It's being clear enough to just simply examine what's serving and what's not serving you, what's serving and what's not serving the greater good, and to choose who to be based on your observations.

Neutrality of mind asks you to step back, observe the situation as it IS without condemning or judging, and begin to consider that in a world full of changing morals, changing beliefs, "right" and "wrong" are simply imaginary human constructs.

The same is true for your own personal beliefs. The next time you encounter a pattern that leaves you feeling guilt or shame, employ the power of a neutral mind. Step outside yourself and observe why you have reached this point so many times. Spend a moment observing the observable—as an impartial observer— and you may just find that your next decision about how you feel will lead you to a more empowered choice in who you next show up as, how you next decide who to be. Nowhere is the power of a neutral mind more effective than in relationship to yourself. It will allow you to literally make quantum leaps in your own personal evolutionary process.

A neutral mind holds no judgment. It condemns nothing and no one, least of all yourself. It simply sees, with open eyes and a tempered heart, how LIFE IS in this inevitable moment.

Just like everything else, neutrality is a simple choice. The more you make the choice to BE neutral, the more you'll begin to see LIFE as IT IS, rather than life as you've colored it with your many judgments and critiques.

> *"Do not judge, and you will*
> *never be mistaken."*
>
> —*Rousseau*

Note to self...

Practice being neutral consistently.

Your neutrality will serve you
in developing the willingness to
become the changes you seek.

From Wherever You Are
to Being Neutral

What is your most prevalent feeling, right now, in your heart? What are your prevailing emotions? Is it guilt? Shame? Anger? Anxiety? Or perhaps you're living with pride, on your way to being courageously vulnerable enough to create your life as you choose it to be. Whatever it is and where ever you are, please get that you're okay. It's okay to be who you are, and it's okay to feel as you feel. Is this clear?

Because it's essential to feel, completely, whatever your prevailing emotion is. Whatever emotion you have in a moment, feel it until you complete it. You can complete only that which you allow yourself to feel completely. Once complete, you are able to move on. It's only until you come complete with your feelings that you can move into neutrality with clear, uncompromising choice.

Understand that no one emotion is "better" than another. After all, what is IS. Yet, your desire to evolve requires that you become complete with any outstanding emotions and feelings. Your personal evolution will be thwarted if you are unable to feel your feelings to completion; and you will again turn back to your patterns of self medication, distractions, and numbing.

The Map of Consciousness, as illustrated in David Hawkins' book *Power vs. Force*, is an illustrative chart to map your conscious evolution. It's also a powerful living poem for humanity and its evolutionary process. For more information on where to find the Map, see the resource center at *http://www.WithInAsThru.com/thehandbook/resources.*

For the purpose of this discussion, just understand that the lowest level on the map is shame, with guilt just above it, apathy next moving through grief and fear and so on until you get to courage. From courage, it's a quantum leap into neutrality. Once neutrality is reached, you'll find it easier and easier to evolve from willingness and acceptance up through reason, love and joy. The highest level of the map is enlightenment, the evolutionary goal for each individual seeker.

The important thing to remember is that there's no need to get stuck in any one level of consciousness. In fact, getting stuck is perhaps the most detrimental thing you can do on your journey. If you feel guilt, you might first need to feel grief or fear in order to get out of the stuckedness of guilt. You might need to feel pride in order to stop living a pattern of unfulfilling desires.

"She laid down in her party dress and never got up
Needless to say she missed the party
She just got sad
Then she got stuck"
—Ani Difranco, "Slide"

Wherever you are on this map, neutrality IS your initial event horizon; however, it's important that you honor all emotions in between—as once you truly understand neutrality, you can move ever higher up the scale with ease.

Remember that reluctance in moving past any of these emotions is evidence that you have wounds that have not yet been healed, wounds that perhaps keep you trapped in yesterday patterns. Where there is a pattern, there is a choice. When you feel any reluctance to evolve your consciousness, observe the observable even as you feel to completion your feelings. FEEL THEM as deeply as you possibly can. Only then can you begin to move truly into neutrality, letting go of yesterday patterns for tomorrow choices, made now in this inevitable moment.

Choose,
without judgment.

observe pattern,
then shift,
jump into the river of experience,
keep jumping into play,
until new choices,
become you.

The Question

Who are you?

Your answer IS your choice, your life to live as you so choose.

> *"Be who you are and say what you feel, because those who mind don't matter, and those who matter don't mind."*
>
> —Dr. Seuss

Whether you're aware of this or not, conscious of this or not, this one question is the beginning and end point to your every experience in this now inevitable moment. And it would serve you to add some further considerations here, if you're so willing.

Are you willingness enough to be who you know Self to Be?

Say YES! Begin again right here and now. Just think about it for a moment and really ask yourself, "Who am I? What is my purpose in being who I am?"

Now, before you answer, consider that you're not your mother or your father. You're not your spouse or significant other. You're not your brother or sister. You're not your grandparents or elders. You're not your children. You're not your roles, your functions, your responsibilities, your titles, your money, or your clothes. You're not the things you say or the things you do, although that's how you're best known. And by your fruits you are known. But you're not even your fruits.

You're not your name and you're not your body. So, ask again, "Who am I? And who am I BEing right now, in this inevitable moment?"

Why have you come? Why did you choose to reenter space-time? Why did you choose the parents you chose? Do you remember?

Are you willing to be responsible in having chosen them? Surely you must remember, at least in glimpses? What are your passions, your interests, your joys, your loves?

Become willingness enough to engage free will. Reclaim your divine-right of choice. WithInAsThru your choice to BE, BE IT! Be willingness enough to change the only thing in your power— your true power—yourself.

This is the beginning again. This is where you get to forgive your perceived past. Not by force. Not through command and demand energy. Not via the negative self-speak pattern that has lived with you for far too long.

Where there is a pattern, there is choice. Choose to be willingness enough to release blame, complain, explain, attack, and defense forever.

Because you're not your mother and you're not your father; and you're not your children. You're not your job, your work, your title, or your roles. You're not the identities or masks you put on. You're not the things you do or the clothes you wear. You're not the car you drive or the wittiness you bring to an evening. You're certainly not what you buy. Yet this question lives eternally present, far beyond your identities and your roles. "Who are you?"

Note to self...

Who are you?
Your ever evolving answer IS your life,
as you live IT, exactly as IT IS.

Practice Self-Coding

Write Your Living I AM Poem

So, who are you? Isn't this a much more interesting question than your typical, "What do you do?"

The purpose of the I AM Poem process is to help steward you as deep as you're willing to go with the one question you're ever being answer to, "Who Am I?"

The I AM Poem is a tool, a process of creative choice, if you will, to help you creatively choose who you are and who you're choosing to become. It puts in to play the considerations offered here such that, once applied, you embody your poem. You'll come to live on purpose, completely at choice, the poem you script.

The poem you write, only you can become.

> *"Every single soul is a poem. It's written on the back of God's hand."*
> —*Michael Franti and Spearhead, "Every Single Soul"*

Just consider the possibility that life has no meaning save the meaning you give it. You have no purpose unless and until you choose a purpose to be, to live. Once you arrive to this consideration withinasthru your own experience, it becomes a much clearer possibility to consider, "that nothing in life is ever just happening to you, your life as you choose it to be, is occurring withinasthru you."

But what is the process by which you're actively and creatively scripting who you are in this inevitable moment? If left unscripted who have you discharged the obligation to? Your parents? Your cultural norms? Television? Who? What?

If you choose to live life on purpose, you must become willingness enough to give meaning to your life by writing your own purpose, by coding yourself. This is not a chicken or egg invitation. It's yet another clarity point that you are eternally at choice in the matter and form of your life.

There is no more important work that you'll ever do than to declare and become who you desire to be. As you choose, so too will you become, aware or unaware—conscious or unconscious. Be aware. Elevate your conscious ability to choose. Live life on purpose, at choice. Be you.

Gratitude for who you are, be then your certainty in the process of scripting your "I AM Poem." Withinasthru this process, a process that is intended to be a living one, you'll continually renew and script who you are and who you're choosing to become. Meaning, it's a poem you'll never stop writing and becoming. You'll come often to its inspired guidance for reference and renewal. You'll come to your I AM Poem to recreate yourself—rewriting, adding to, deleting from, swirling up new possibilities to be and become—because it'll become the reflective words of your soul and soul's purpose. It'll become the primary tool to help steward you upon your own evolution in a way that eternally moves, touches and inspires you to ever greater Self experiences and expressions.

The I AM Poem Process is available at the WithInAsThru web site: *http://www.WithInAsThru.com/IAMPoem.*

Note to self...

> This life you live, you get to choose IT.
> You're making it up.
> Make it worthy of you and your dreams.

Why Did You Choose Your Parents?

Why did you choose your parents? This is a very empowering question. It's empowering for two reasons. First, you must be able to consider the possibility that you did, in fact, choose your parents. Are you ready and willing to consider this possibility? Because it's certainly not a given, is it?

Secondly, this question asks you to believe something that maybe you didn't before. It asks you to at least consider something possible that perhaps you didn't consider possible a moment ago.

What would it look like and feel like to you if you knew, beyond a shadow of a doubt, that you did choose your parents; and you chose them consciously, even purposely? You chose them for all the reasons that you love them today. You chose them for all the reasons you might judge them today. You chose them as a base cause for much of the pain and suffering you still walk around with as your story, as your drama. You chose them for who they are and what they taught you. Some of you even chose them because of their utter lack of parenting. Thus, you are that you are.

> "...there's a story behind everything. How a picture got on a wall. How a scar got on your face. Sometimes the stories are simple, and sometimes they are hard and heartbreaking. But behind all your stories is always your mother's story, because hers is where yours begins."
> —Mitch Albom, "for one more day"

Although you may not, in this moment, remember that this is what's so, you did choose your parents. And they chose you, as well. As is often the case, this thought may initially confuse you. It may enrage you, bringing to surface every wound that you might blame upon your parents. Your process is perfect. Feel completely what is coming for you. That which you allow yourself to feel, you'll soon be able to complete.

The truth is, you may not be ready to accept this consideration at this time. If this is what's so for you, this is okay as well. Your resistance to what is will continue to allow you to feel the anger or the shame or the guilt or whatever suffering you're still choosing to hold on to. Again, you're always at choice in the matter of your life. And where there's a pattern, there's a choice.

However, your drama is already beginning to close around you, even as you read this. Right now you're asking a different question. You're getting to try on a new consideration. What if your suffering is simply part of a larger identity you've worn for so long that you've actually begun to feel that this identity is who you really are? What then?

What do you do now, if your preconceived self-notion isn't so? Who are you if not your stories of suffering and misery? It could be that you're initially more afraid of letting go of the identity of suffering than excited by the prospect that this is not who you really are.

You're perhaps more afraid to let go of your stories than excited by the opportunity of beginning to script a new, more empowered one. This is understandable. This can even be said to be normal, though not necessarily natural.

So, please, hold on to your stories of misery and suffering for as long as you feel justified in doing so. Again, as a simple consideration for your process, please simply know that you are, as in every other aspect of LIFE, at choice in the matter of IT.

When you bemoan your experiences with your parents, observe carefully the words that you're using to tell your story of suffering. As you observe your story, you'll be much more aware of the fragility by which your story of suffering exists. And you'll be even clearer that your story of suffering exists because you're choosing IT to exist. Its presence, its distracting gifts, are literally in existence because you've chosen to give them existence.

When you're ready for the stories of suffering to disappear from your life, especially the stories you continue to blame upon your parents, you need only remember that you are its source of existence. As you choose it to live withinasthru each feeling's appearance, you'll come to get that you are its only source of disappearance. Not the circumstances or the events that occurred, but you're always at choice in the way you feel in relationship to the circumstances or events.

Note to self...

Come to see your parents as one of your clearest choices made, and you will heal all that you would have suffered about them a moment before.

What are Your Parents' Reflective Patterns?

Perhaps your mother was very controlling. Perhaps your father was aloof, or not even around as you were growing up. Perhaps the opposite is true for you. Regardless, your parents' patterns, the ones you remember them by today, are called "reflective patterns".

Recognizing your parents' reflective patterns allows you to face the judgment you may have of them. What is it that you judge most about your parents? Because what you judge most about your parents lives withinasthru you, or it couldn't exist in any moment you are. This is generationally what's so.

Recall the passage in the Bible that says, "…visiting the iniquity of fathers on the children and on the grandchildren to the third and fourth generations." Instead of viewing this as a spiteful God, perhaps you might consider a more loving interpretation? Consider that the reflective patterns of ego—judgment, aloofness, controlling traits, anger, etc.—are passed on from generation to generation, until one person (and this would be you) is brave enough to stand in the fire of Self transformation and say, "I accept what is and choose to suffer the misperceptions of my family no more."

When you find the courage to let go of these reflective patterns, these toxic beliefs and traits, you're able then to heal them in your parents, as well as all of the generations that come before and after you.

Be the courageous vulnerability to really examine your feelings for your parents from a neutral perspective. Get that what you judge about them is what you're resisting most in identifying within yourself. Once you get to a point where you're willing to shred off these identities, these beliefs, you realize that, from an evolutionary perspective, your parents are who they are because you have chosen them for the gifts that they give while being who they are. There's nothing to fix about them, or the past. There is no wrong to right, no bad to make good. They simply are who they are—and you are who you in so many ways because they are who they are.

Note to self...

Choose to accept your parents as they are.
Experience what it feels like to feel complete
in relationship to your parents.

Courage to Transcend DNA

Perhaps the biggest challenge you'll face in your journey is finding the ability to transcend your core DNA, or the misperceptions your ancestors died with that still live withinasthru you.

Take a look at yourself, your parents, and your parents' parents. What misperceptions lived withinasthru them? What energy leaking patterns of misperception have you observed in yourself and your ancestors?

> "If you look deeply into the palm of your hand,
> You will see your parents and all generations of
> your ancestors. All of them are alive in this mo-
> ment. Each is present in your body. You are the
> continuation of each of these people."
> —Thich Nhat Hanh

As you begin to own your feelings, you'll come to realize that how you feel about What IS is in direct relationship to how you experience LIFE. Most of the paths to perception were taught to you by your parents and grandparents. And they were, in turn, taught by their parents and grandparents. The truth of this process lives forever within you. It is you until such time that you're willingness enough to observe the patterns of perception that rule your life and make a new choice. How do you come to observe these patterns? In your willingness to be in your silence, come to be with what and how you feel.

The more you're able to get present to how you feel about what is true for you, the more powerful your abilities to observe the observable become. As you come to observe patterns that serve you, you'll choose to strengthen them. The ones that are no longer serving you, you'll probably desire to release. This is a very positive sign that you are evolving, that you are being and becoming the change that a moment before you sought in external ways.

This is ever clear in your role as a parent as you come to observe transference. Transference is the act or process of transferring ownership. In parenting, transference is shifting emotions or desires originally associated withinasthru you to that of your child. The father who didn't make varsity pushes his son to become the football hero. Or the mother who isn't self aware of the habits by which she lives judges her daughter when she practices the very same habits in her own way.

Transference, as you come to remember, is a generational reality. A reality that lives withinasthru your very DNA.

Although science may have not yet proven what is about to be offered here, it won't be much longer until it does. In all likelihood, it's already proven that when you reassociate painful memories of suffering—in relationship to your family members—into new associations that empower and inspire you, you cause a measurable shift both up and down your family tree.

Where, a moment ago, you blamed your mother for something you felt missing from your childhood, you come to this inevitable moment, knowing IT wasn't missing at all. Then something in both you and your mother is healed, permanently. The misperception of suffering is bridged eternally withinasthru your choice to accept what is as What IS. In doing so, you release needless suffering from your life. Your life lived then becomes the basis of your prodigy.

Coming to this conclusion may take real forgiveness. It may take months of process as you choose to embody it. But the moment that the actual shift occurs, ripples of effect are indelibly scripted withinasthru three generations being and living this new possibility.

A mother who forgives herself her bad habits notices instantly that the habits reflecting in her daughter have miraculously disappeared, as has her anger towards her own mother been forgiven.

The miracle is in the remembrance that there is but one energy, one information, and one intelligence that IS your family, that IS all of LIFE. As you take ownership for your life as it is, you come to heal all the misperceptions that live within your genealogy. Learn to use forgiveness as one of the most powerful tools to feel good in relationship to your parents or your role as parent.

Whatever lives in you as a story of suffering or misery withinasthru the way you were parented, or the way in which you parent, come to see IT through eyes of forgiveness. Where forgiveness is not possible yet, simply see it withinasthru eyes that observe the observable. See it as an occurrence that could be forgiven someday, when you're ready and willing.

Let the power of forgiveness help you let go of needless suffering withinasthru your experience of family, especially in relationship to those who raised you and those whom you raised or are raising. There is no more important work than your role as parent.

> *"Every decision you make, IS a choice between a grievance and a miracle. Release*

all grievances, resentments and regrets; And choose the miracle."

— *A Course in Miracles*

Note to self...

> Be willingness enough to release all your grievances, resentments and regrets.
> Be the miracle and transcend your very DNA.

What or Who Do You Judge Most?

G o deep here. Remember the last time you judged another person. Maybe it was your spouse or your parents for not "being there" enough for you. Perhaps, it was your coworker for slacking off. It may have been someone you saw on television, or a celebrity.

As challenging as this may be to consider, simply seek to determine what is your truth withinasthru this consideration and live IT. No other request truly lives on the pages of this handbook.

So, if you are willingness enough, consider that which you judge most in another exists withinasthru you, or it couldn't exist in any moment you are. Because what you judge in another is, at some level, what you're resisting most in identifying within yourself.

> *"...that which you judge most in another,*
> *exists withinasthru you,*
> *or it couldn't exist,*
> *in any moment you are."*

By this logic, if you judge the people around you to be frivolous with their money, always spending it crazily, it's because somewhere you don't yet have mastery of money and most likely are spending it frivolously or have overcompensated by becoming too frugal. Either way, if you're judging people because their habits offend you, it's because, at some level, you too have similar habits, regardless of the form by which you bring your perceptions into your living experience.

Perhaps your way of committing to being "not that" which you're judging is by condemning others who "are that". Still, you're much more committed to what you're not than who you are. This is where you'll do well in giving up the crutch of "us/them" perceptions, returning again to your awareness that you are that you are. Conduct the "I Am THAT I Am" experiment as often as is necessary to see and know that you are that which you're judging.

> *"When you judge another, you don't define them, you define yourself."*
>
> —*Wayne Dyer*

Be not afraid of embracing the idea that you are who and what you judge. Be aware of any pattern in which you ask others to judge and condemn another, as this is the root of gossip. The roots of gossip are Self judgment, using others as contrast to allow your justifications more validity.

Release any such crutches. They are of no use to you now. In truth, crutches merely enable you to live without self-awareness, and keep you from living your dreams true. Any use of the crutch of judgment, condemnation, or gossip is an opportunity to embrace your own shadows.

> *"Instead of criticizing others (no matter how much they may deserve it), I allow myself to devote my time to the discovery of traits of my*

> *own, which need be correct lest they provide*
> *the basis of just criticism against me."*
> —*Napoleon Hill*

The way to come complete with any pattern of judgment is to acknowledge your shadows. Then honor them for the many roles they've played in helping you create diverse experiences in fully experiencing who you are. In your past, you may have consciously run from your shadows into what you perceived to be light. Chances are good that you're still running today.

However, every time you run from your shadows into perceived light, you're actually just running around in the dark. It's not until you embrace the shadow AS that part of you that IS shadow that you're able to employ its service in being the light that you are. For is it not light that creates shadows? Is LIFE not the everything and the nothing? Fear not, then, your nothingness. Embrace the truth that you are a no body. When you accept completely that you are a no body, you, in this inevitable moment, become some body, both form and matter.

> *"It is our light, not our darkness,*
> *that most frightens us."*
> —*Marianne Williamson*

Be an entire sphere of LIFE that you are. All that you would perceive to be, good and bad, you are. Release your judgments—those you have of other people and those you have of yourself—to experience more fully the complete sphere of LIFE that you are. Because when you let go of your judgments, you let go of the need to keep them in existence.

Note to self...

> Whatever you judge lives in you or it
> couldn't exist in any moment you are.

Release Blame Patterns

*B*lame is a function of judgment. Consider that the deeper roots of blame exist because somewhere you have guilt or anger that you're projecting upon another. Somewhere you're expecting them to be what you desire them to be, rather than who they really are.

There are few paths to suffering as fast as blame. Blame, as an experience, evaporates personal power. It suctions off life force and will of action due to its roots in separation. Blame is an act of separation. Blame is only possible when seeing another as some other than you.

Whenever you're blaming any occurrence, situation, scenario, anything, or anyone for how you're feeling, (it must be obvious by now) it's really you. And they're simply that part of you that's allowing you the opportunity to be who you are.

> *"You are who you are in*
> *relationship to another."*
> —Neale Donald Walsch, *"Conversations with God"*

Blame patterns allow you to falsely discharge your personal responsibility. Doing so is easy withinasthru the myth of separation. It's also easy when you continue to define responsibility as some kind of "heavy" obligation or burden.

Every man's burden is the heaviest, just ask him.

However, when you come to see the illusion of separation as an illusion, and come to know responsibility as your ability to respond, you might choose to release every pattern of blame you have ever created.

Wherever there is a pattern there is a choice. This is your choice to make withinasthru this inevitable moment. As you choose to release your patterns of blaming others and situations for how you feel, you'll come to naturally apply and expand your understanding of the Golden Rule: "Do unto others as you would have done to you... for there is none other than you." If there is none other than you, then your blame is clearly a projection of your own misperceived lack of ability to respond. Be responsible, able to respond to any person, any situation, any circumstance, being who you are.

> *"You never bring yourself to any moment*
> *you're not fully prepared for..."*
> —*Buddha*

It's an incredibly freeing moment when you begin to let go of these patterns of judgment and blame, to realize that no one has or has ever had control over you. That is, except the control you gave them through your judgments and patterns of blame and complain. Release the patterns, claim your ability to respond. Respond beautifully.

As a simple experiment, come to consider any pattern of judgment or blame to be an opportunity to say and see differently... "Whoa. I'm blaming someone for how I'm feeling. This means, in this inevitable moment, I'm giving away all of my power to this person I'm blaming. If I'm giving all my power to them, how can I be using my powers to live life on purpose? Hmm, I guess I can't. Perhaps there's another way?"

It's at this point, this inevitable moment, where you can employ the wonderful state of neutrality to observe the situation, take your three breaths, and make a new choice. You will strengthen your ability to respond, being who you are, naturally. As you so choose to consider and experiment, so too may your life reflect who you are withinasthru ever expanding beauty and joy.

> Note to self...
>
> Let go of the crutches of blame forever.
> Choose to accept what is rather than suffer it.
> LIFE's much friendlier this way.

Let Go of Complain Patterns

*P*atterns of judgment, blame, complain, attack and defense all serve as an opportunity to reclaim your personal power.

Because, if you're like most people, you find yourself saying things like, "I am so sick of..." "He never listens to me..." "The traffic is always so horrible..." at least every once in awhile, if not quite often.

These are your complain patterns. Complain patterns, just like blame and judgment, are simply ways in which you're allowing yourself to continue needless suffering—at the whims of life as you perceive it now, at the mercy of others, and a helpless party in any given situation—kind of like a victim. While it may seem easier to blame and complain away your problems, you'll never be free of the irritants until you're prepared to own them completely.

Now is the time to let go of all of your victim patterns. The benefits are peace, happiness, and a life that you choose consciously.

Otherwise, your complain patterns will continue to keep you stuck in the quicksand of stagnation—whether it's financial, a relationship, or anything in between—a stagnancy that may not serve you in fulfilling your desires. Release then your judgments, your blame and your complaints.

Consider that the only constant among all of your patterns is you. You're it. And it's always been you. This is because nothing in your life is ever just happening to you. Your life, as you live it, as you choose it to be, exactly as it is in this inevitable moment, is occurring withinasthru you. This is eternally so.

One of the beautiful things you'll come to notice, as you become willingness enough to let go of your patterns that separate you from your power, is that it might be difficult to be around those who judge, blame, and complain a lot. It's not that you don't love them. Quite the opposite, in fact. It's that you've come to love them enough to know them as equal, as simply this part of you that is them. And their reliance on the crutches of perceived separation will feel like a magnet that's rotated to repel your attractant field.

In essence, you'll become repellant to one another. Who you are will not dance the dance of judgment and gossip. You'll no longer be willing to walk on crutches into the dreams of your tomorrow. And if they choose to still be victims to needless suffering, release them completely to the path they choose to walk. Do this as a signature of love. Speak it as a choice to Self. Make room to expand your community experience. Be open to bringing new people into your life who have made similar choices to reclaim their personal power.

Note to self...

You become who you surround yourself with.

Remove Explanations & Justifications from Conversations

his is perhaps repetitive by now. If so, jump ahead. However, it's important to choose to at least consider the subtle nuance of language being offered throughout this handbook. Because you've probably, like most, spent many conversations trying to justify your feelings, your actions, your decisions, it's important to add explain and justification patterns to the list of patterns brought to attention here in this conversation.

"Why explanation? Why justification?" You ask.

Explain energy lacks feeling. It bypasses heart. It seeks to tell you something, asking for your belief or your faith. Explain, as an energy, doesn't readily move, touch, or inspire in its structured language. And justification, well, you probably already get why it's been identified here as a pattern you'll do well to release from your employment.

What else could justification, as a pattern, serve other than to remove you from personal responsibility? It may seem as if you're trying to get another to see "it" your way. But who are you really trying to justify these things to? That's right, yourself!

It's easy to notice when justifications work their way into conversations, or even when you begin entertaining them in your own mind. The energy shifts, and you may feel a twinge of imbalance or "offness".

There's no need to justify anything in your world. If you are the creator of your experience, you have nothing to justify, you have only to choose. Go to the root of your justifications the next time you find them sneaking into conversation. What don't you feel comfortable with? Is there a lie you falsely believe you could keep from this part of you? Could it be a pattern you're ready to recognize, observe, and choose differently about? Could it be that these feelings are opening you up to a new way to being at choice?

Explain energy is a distant cousin to justification. Explain energy is not as strong, but carries a subtle "this is better than that" connotation. This is not to say that explain energy doesn't have its purpose. It does. It serves well in a medical crises where you desire to have information explained to you as concisely as is possible in order to make informed decisions. However, when opting to use explain energy over authentically sharing your personal experiences is where the pattern may not be serving you or your relationships.

Conversations where you authentically share from your heart with another are much more effective than explaining some kind of insight you've come to. When opting to explain, it is ever so easy to fall into the trap of explaining how your beliefs or experiences are somehow better than what another believes or has experienced.

> *"Your way is not a better way.*
> *Their way is not a better way.*
> *Either way IS but another way,*
> *Another way of Being."*

Have you ever observed a conversation that turned sour quickly, but were unaware of what may have caused it to do so? Consider that either you or the person you were in conversation with began to "explain things" to you, or you to them. Nothing sours conversations quicker than false righteousness, either perceived or expressed.

Whenever you feel explain energy coming on, instead just share your heart with whomever you're talking to. Be authentic about your inauthenticities, your patterns of judgment, blame, complain, explain or justification. Such authentic conversations help to avoid needless conflicts. Inspired conversations invent inspired possibilities.

How does such a shift occur? It occurs by simply saying (or even silently recognizing), "Look. A moment ago I was being pompous by thinking I was telling you something you didn't know. I apologize, and I ask your forgiveness. Let me instead share with you my experience and give you the fresh seeing and listening you've come here to receive. Let us grow and learn together."

> "If you believe in peace, act peacefully; if you believe in love, acting lovingly; if you believe every which way, then act every which way,— that's perfectly valid—but don't go out trying to sell your beliefs to the system. You end up contradicting what you profess to believe in, and you set a bum example. If you want to change the world, change yourself."
>
> —Tom Robbins, "Still Life with Woodpecker"

Note to self...

Your opportunity here is to experience IT your way.

Share your experiences openly, authentically, and transparently.

Attack No One, Least of All Self

When the early warning patterns of judgment, blame, complain, explain and justification aren't addressed, it is most likely that you'll choose anger, perhaps even attack. Because when you're feeling angry or resentful, it may be your first instinct to jump in and attack someone for it—maybe even yourself. Attacking carries basically the same energy as the other opportunity patterns, but is much more volatile. Attack energy easily becomes violent. Violent thoughts breed violent words. Violent words bring violent actions. Violence is much easier to succumb to when you've allowed your patterns of blame to become emotionally charged.

> *"I don't want to be one the battles
> always choose,*
>
> *Because inside I realize that
> I'm the one confused...*
>
> *I don't know what's worth fighting
> for or why I had to scream,*
>
> *I don't know why I instigate and
> say what I don't mean,*
>
> *I don't know how I got this way,
> I know it's not alright,*
>
> *So, I'm breaking the habit... tonight."*
> —*Linkin Park, "Breaking the Habit"*

For example, perhaps you're in a relationship and your significant other comes home late. You've been waiting for hours, playing over and over in your mind all the things he was doing while out of the house. He walks in to your emotionally charged judgments, as you begin to attack him through a barrage of questions—"Where have you been? You said you were going to be home at 8:00. It's 9:30. I bet you had to work late again because of her, didn't you? I can't believe you'd make me wait like this. You're so selfish." And you attack him, even though your state of being has not one thing to do with him, regardless of why he is late or what he was doing with whom.

Your feelings are your feelings. How you choose to feel is a choice only you can make. When you choose to attack, it's because you feel wronged or damaged. But for you to feel wronged or damaged, you must first willingly give your power to the person you feel has wronged you.

Again, attack is the action of blame. When you choose to attack, withinasthru this inevitable moment, you're choosing to embody and make real the illusion of separation. Because this moment is inevitable, you have but one simple choice present: accept IT or suffer IT. When you make any illusion of separation real, you choose suffering. When your suffering becomes unbearable, your desire twists further down the illusionary spiral of separation. The further you twist and contort your suffering into your experienced reality, the more readily you desire others to suffer with you. This is perhaps why you attack those you claim to love most.

It's ironic that you don't choose to see What IS seeable in suffered moments. It is easy to see that your choice to accept or suffer this inevitable moment is connected, at root, to who you're choosing to be in relationship to LIFE. As you choose to be, so too is your experience. As you experience, so too do you come to know you to be as you experience yourself.

IT IS obvious to any outside observer that you're the only constant. The irony is that when it's easiest to observe the foolishness of any pattern that separates you from every moment you are, it's the moment you create the very experience of being separate.

Knowing this is so doesn't matter, or doesn't materialize, unless and until you act upon what you know. Knowledge applied is wisdom. Come to see and know, then, that attack is an opportunity, a magnificent opportunity, to begin to let go of your separation pattern. Because of its emotionally charged nature, it brings you to the brink of realizing "I Am THAT I Am!" so much faster.

Not surprisingly, the same is true in relationship to any pattern of attacking yourself. In a moment of perceived failure, you may say to yourself, "I am so stupid! Why don't I ever get things right? I don't even deserve to be happy. I don't deserve to live." And other such nonsense. Well, it goes without saying that these forms of attack patterns will never serve you in an expansive way. They'll not aide you in your desire to live as you consciously choose to live. Remember to see and know, "I Am THAT I Am."

Do you choose to attack yourself this way? Do you choose to be the words you use for yourself in these moments? Or are you willingness enough to breathe, smile, and feel grateful for a new way, a new you, forever leaving these patterns behind?

"As you choose to BE, so too IS your experience."

Choose to release any and all attack patterns. Let your life lived serve as an example of what it means to truly live non-violently. Use the inspiration offered here. Expand these inspired words into even deeper meaning.

"We may never be strong enough to be entirely nonviolent—in thought, word and deed. But

we must keep nonviolence as our goal and
make strong progress towards it."

—Mohandas Gandhi

Nothing to Defend, What Is, IS

The illusion of separation gives you many gifts. It gives you the right to judge, condemn, blame, complain, attack and defend. It gives you the experience of being right and making others wrong. It helps you justify decisions that no longer serve you or the greater good. The illusion's greatest gift of all is its allowance, its cause into existence, an experience that somehow you've come to rely on completely. The illusion of separation makes possible an experience you've come to see and know as "us" and "them".

Now, you may already be smiling at some level, humbled in the reflection such directness inspires. Be willingness enough to further consider that these so called "gifts" are the essential ingredients to war of any size.

To this end, ask yourself this question, "Would there be anything to defend, ever, if the myths of separation dissolved? Would there be any thought of, much less an experience of war, if I knew that the truest justice I'll ever come to know arrives withinasthru my choice to see and know 'Just Us'?"

Would there ever be reason for defense against this part of you that is them?

No, there would not.

It's only because you perpetuate the illusion of separation that a stance of defense is even possible. When is defense necessary?

When you feel as if someone is attacking you, your defense mechanism is activated. The circle of attack and defense is the reason that war has perpetuated itself upon your entire experience of life on Earth. War's not only unfortunate, it's unnecessary. Worse, its ineffectiveness is obvious. You've proven, both personally and collectively, beyond need of further experimentation, war does not work in order to create peace.

But then, war wasn't invented to create peace, was it? Indeed not. It was created to perpetuate the myth of separation. And this it does exceedingly well.

> *"Seek not peace here; but find it everywhere."*
> —James Twyman, *The Beloved Community*

In reality, what possible reason could you have ever had in creating war, if your clearest intention was peace? What justification could you possibly hallucinate for attacking another, any other, if you knew all others to be that part of LIFE that is them? Would there ever be possibility of defense without first creating the possibility of attack? There could not be.

Let any experience of "Us/Them" be an opportunity to see "Just Us". As you choose to see "Just Us", you'll come to experience a clearer understanding of what true justice may look like. What is LIFE, IS. Choose to see LIFE as IT IS.

"But," you might say, "we need to defend our homes, we need to defend our families from the enemies out there. Hasn't history shown us this? Don't the terrorist attacks prove this to be what's so?"

Again, as you choose to be, so too do you experience. Meaning, that as you continue to choose to see and know separation to be what is, so too will you continue to create experiences of separation, thereby, once again, justifying your every reason to war. This is because for millennia, the majority of you haven't been willingness enough to be and live as co-creators with LIFE. You've been unwilling to be what you are, one with everything that IS LIFE.

Yet, more and more, studies are proving the interconnectedness of LIFE withinasthru scientific process. Observing the observable, scientists are coming to the same conclusions that mystics have offered throughout recorded history. As a result, humanity is increasing its active participation in the conscious evolution as LIFE experienced on Earth.

When you come to see and know "Just Us" as what is so; when you come to see and know your Self as this part of LIFE that is you; and when you choose to release any myth that has you spinning in patterns of separation, you'll come to experience LIFE as IT IS.

Withinasthru this inevitable moment, choose to no longer suffer any myth that has you separate from LIFE or from one another. Now that you know there's another, isn't it worth at least experimenting with the possibility of employing your personal power rather than giving it away to whomever you would judge or blame? Isn't it an attractive enough consideration to choose to accept What IS as IT IS, rather than to suffer IT?

Breathe. Smile. Feel grateful. Repeat as you may require to become willingness enough to release your every pattern of separation. Judge nothing and no one. Release blame. Let go of complain. Replace explain with authentic sharing. Remove any justifications from conversations. Attack no one, least of all Self. Discharge defense its authority to preemptively attack another, further separating you from LIFE. Know you are at choice whenever and however you observe any form of these patters.

Where there is a pattern, there is a choice.

Note to self...

Release any myth that has you separate
from LIFE or from one another.

say "no" no more
to what IS.

Release judging,
blaming,
complaining,
explaining,
justifying,
attacking,
defending...

feel.

BE.

get quiet,
get honest,
realize you're the answer
to every question
you've ever asked.

your life
is occurring
withinasthru you
this inevitable moment
you are.

Your Insatiable Need to Be Right

What if you knew that you are always right? Would that change the way you looked at things, people, situations? It should, because you are. You are always right—when it comes to your own beliefs, and your own decisions. However, this knowledge runs true in infinite directions and applies to all people. They, too, are always right when it comes to their beliefs, their decisions, whoever you're experiencing as "they".

Consider, if you will, that no one ever sees or knows themselves as "wrong," or does anything wrong for that matter, based upon their model of LIFE. Do you? Do you ever see yourself as wrong, really wrong, based upon your model of LIFE?

This is not to suggest that you don't perhaps choose differently based upon self observation or assessment. Or that you don't, upon Self reflection, ask forgiveness if your actions or ways allowed another to perceive them self as harmed in some way.

What is being offered here is integral to your process of letting go of any false needs you might have of being right at the cost of your happiness.

The important questions to ask then are not, "Who's Right? Who's wrong?" Instead, the discerning question is, "Does this belief serve me and the greater good? Will my decision in this inevitable moment serve me and others?"

> *"Too set in our ways to try to rearrange,*
> *too right to be wrong..."*
> —*Bono of U2, "Like a Song"*

Because the insatiable need to be right is what's created wars, caused families to be torn apart, and led to most of the miseries you see in the world today. Because so many of you have been so inextricably attached to being "right" as you would define "rightness," you've murdered, maimed, and made miserable for millennia human beings with different beliefs, those who have chosen other ways of being human or ways of living life.

Consider where the root cause of the need to be right lies. It lies in the fear of being wrong. The last time you had an argument with a loved one, what was the cause of it? One or both of you needed to be right, because if you weren't right, it meant the other one was—which, by default, would have made you wrong.

> "I won every argument I was in, not by being
> right, but by making the other wrong."
> —Nick Naylor, "Thank You For Smoking"

Consider that you're right and everyone else is too, not because anyone is really either right or wrong, but because there is only one of you in conversation. Release this insatiable need to be right as you will. When you begin to experience only one of you in conversation, you'll come to see the futility in old patterns of needing to be right.

> "There ain't no good guy. There ain't no bad guy.
> There's only you and me and we just disagree."
> —Dave Mason, "We Just Disagree"

Letting Go of Your Need to Be Right

*B*egin, right now, to let go of your need to be right. Consider healing any false misperceptions that keep you separate. Allow these words to guide you into an ever deepening experience of who you really are. Consider this possibility home to your heart.

Go back and remember the last argument you had. Who was it with? What was it even about? Do you remember? Get there. Feel what you felt when you were immersed in the argument. Be again insatiable with your need to be right. Are you there? Good.

Now imagine it differently. Imagine what might have happened had you not felt the need to make the other wrong. Imagine listening to their opinions with consideration, understanding that their "right" was right for them. Can you see a different outcome? Can you feel the understanding and the expansion into a new aspect of your relationship? Is it possible that you could give them the same listening you desire to receive without having to make what they offer right or wrong? Is it at least possible that you could consider doing this?

As you learn to release your addiction to needing to be right, you'll come to experience yourself more and more able to observe the observable. This is a shortcut to your personal growth, a fast track to your conscious evolution. This is what it means to have neutrality of mind. And as you come to more naturally choose neutrality as your way, you'll come to experience a certain joy in your willingness to give others the listening you desire to receive.

Again, most of your conflicts and patterns of suffering will disappear the moment you are willingness enough to give the listening you seek to receive. More often than not, it wouldn't even matter to you if your thoughts or ideas were even used. All that would matter to you is that you received the listening you desired and deserved.

What was, a moment before, a problem or a challenge, now becomes a window of opportunity. This is as true of you in your personal relationships as it is in relationship to your international ones.

Expand this thought now to the macro, and consider how much different the world would be if governments, through the ages, hadn't felt the need to be right at the expense of others' beliefs. It would have been the first step into peace, into conscious understanding between all humans, into unity.

Humanity has this opportunity now, and it begins with you. It always begins with you, because you are every moment you are. As you are, so too is this part of LIFE that is your experience. As more and more of you choose this experience, so too does LIFE reflect your choice. Perhaps this is what is meant in the words withinasthru Gandhi,

"Be the change you desire to see in the world."

And So IT IS.

> Note to self...
> **Release any need to be right.**
> **You'll be happy you did.**

Forgiveness

*G*ratitude is the core of your magnetic attractant field by which your life, as you live it, is occurring withinasthru you. When your ability to be grateful is thwarted somehow, it's usually because you're resisting What IS in some form and have chosen to suffer this inevitable moment.

You may have very real experiences of someone having caused you pain. You may not be ready to forgive just yet. Your process is whole and complete as it is. Just know that resisting any request for forgiveness, whether the request is coming from another or from within your own heart, keeps suffering present in your life.

How do you release suffering and misery? You become willingness enough to forgive the forgivable. Whatever suffering exists, exists only within the illusion of separation, exists only from a thought that has you separate from the one you imagine you are to forgive.

"You can clear all of your karma in an instant, The instant you choose to forgive your self completely."

The key to forgiveness is this—in every single moment, every instance, every disagreement—when you forgive, you are forgiving yourself. This may be hard to digest right now if you're still carrying around a lot of anger and resentment towards another. However, if you're willing to consider the possibility that "there is no one but you," you're ready to make use of the power of forgiveness.

Be willingness enough to go courageously to the root of your emotional pain-body. What experiences of suffering live within its folds? What stories of misery do you keep alive in its field? Ask yourself, "Do I wish those experiences of suffering to repeat themselves?" "Do these stories of misery serve me and the greater good?" If yes, expand them. Give them life. Bring them up for one final experience, rich enough in texture for you to complete this cycle forever.

Otherwise, choose now, in this inevitable moment, to forgive and let go.

Forgiveness is a catalyst to gratitude. Its use reflects and expands your choice to live life, as you choose it to be, on purpose.

"Life is an adventure in forgiveness."

—*Norman Cousins*

Note to self...

Forgiveness is a catalyst to gratitude.
Use it expand your choice to live LIFE,
as you choose IT to BE, on purpose.

Practice of Tending Self Garden

Spend some time here to assess your state of Being. Who are you being in most moments that matter? Who are you generally known to be? How do you tend to show up? What are your patterns of perception? Who are you being right now?

View yourself wholly and completely. See where you've been loving recently, where you've judged, and where you've felt disappointment or fear. Visualize your current state of emotion as a beautiful garden, full of all kinds of foliage, flowers, and plants.

Now imagine the spaces where you've been less than loving, less than complete, as weeds. A moment in which you judged a friend, you might choose to see as a thistle. A moment in which you blamed your mother for your actions today, you might see as a dandelion or some other form of weed.

You know what happens when you leave weeds untended, don't you? They grow and multiply and take over an entire garden. This is what your patterns of separation will do if you don't tend them. Find the weeds within yourself. Identify them and examine them. You may want to pull them out before they cause damage to other parts of your garden.

However, tending your garden doesn't just include pulling out weeds, does it? A garden needs care and nurturing—this is where self silence and empowering perceptions come to your aide. For as you remove each weed through forgiveness, you replace it with a more reflective addition. Perhaps a lilac or a fragrant rosebush more clearly reflects who you are? You're always at choice to create your garden as you will.

Let the sun shine on every part of your garden, illuminating it with neutrality. Where there's a weed hiding in the shadows, expand the LIFE sphere you would more fully encompass in the area still fertile for weeds. Don't judge the weeds. Simply observe them and thank them for their gift of feeling. Feel them to completion even as you choose to forgive them. You'll notice as you do this, it transforms and blossoms, enriching the vast array of your garden within.

Practice this as often as may be necessary to tend your garden. A garden needs continuous care to flourish. Plant new seeds all the time, seeds that serve you, seeds that serve the greater good. Find silent time each day to tend your garden. Your garden is your place to heal in moments of pain or disappointment. From here, you can weed as necessary, or simply spend time viewing the rich, vast, beautiful flora you planted long ago that today sustains you.

Note to self...
> Be completely grateful for all your garden has become over the years...
> Keep IT vibrant. Allow IT to grow and flourish.
> Tend to IT often.

Clear

Choice

Intention

Ask

Grateful

Giving

Receptive

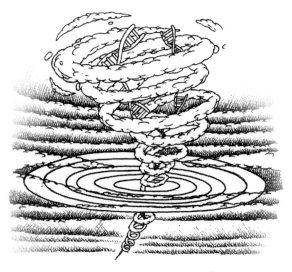

Intention

What does IT Mean to BE Intentional?

Who, in this inevitable moment, do you choose to be? What do you choose to do? What do you choose to have? Withinasthru your clearest values, what do you choose to experience in your life, as your life? As you answer these questions, you're automatically setting an intention. Being intentional is a necessary step in your journey to becoming who you desire to become.

Once you've established the premise that everything is occurring withinasthru you at the energy, information, and intelligence level, it means that anything you ever think of already exists. As you focus your intention on a single thought, you mix desire energy with thought energy—the two first necessary components to bringing, through the universe, what you're asking for.

As you set an intention, as you focus on who you choose to be, whether it's creativity, loving or artistic, and you mix your intention with gratitude, you can release the intention to the universe. In this inevitable moment, you know that what you desire is already forming into existence, is already on its way to your experience. Now experience gratitude for its existence. And so it is.

Additionally, there's another important component to being intentional. Intention is that state of being you hold for your own possibility. It's your clearest desire to experience your values withinasthru your life lived. Attention to your intention must come in to play; otherwise, your intentions will disappear to the winds of swirling desires.

Intention is the event horizon of who you desire to be and become. You set your intention withinasthru your values and ask for the experiences by which you'll begin to expand in spherical ways. Once set, allow your gratitude to work as the electromagnetic attractant, assisting LIFE in its natural process of giving you the very experiences you have asked to receive.

Attention is what you focus on in the here, now, and in-betweens. So if you say to the universe, "I desire the experience of being abundance withinasthru the experience of being an entrepreneur," it's clear that your own business, part and parcel, won't show up to you without any attention to this desire, or without the necessary actions to help you choose the experience of being abundance as an entrepreneur. You get to become that which you intend to experience.

As you begin to feel comfortable being intentional, you'll also notice a flip-switch. You'll become really clear on what your values are, you'll become very clear on who you desire to be in this world, what you desire to do and then what you desire to have. By focusing first on being the experience of that which you desire, rather than having it, you'll automatically begin to do what a person who is being the experience does.

For example, if you're intentional about experiencing love, then by the very direct act of "being love" you become the love you sought a moment before, a love you somehow imagined you were lacking.

As you choose to be the experience you desire to receive, your process of intention will effortlessly flow. And it begins by getting clearly intentional about your values.

> *"Our intention creates our reality."*
> —Wayne Dyer

What do you Value Most in Life?

Ask yourself this question, "What do I value most in life?"

What is it? What is your primary value that influences every choice you make as to who you are? Is it love? Is it adventure? Is it abundance? What do you value more than anything? Contribution? Joy? Freedom?

Values are felt. Determining your primary motivation is a part of your emotional body. It's the sponsoring cause to who you are in relationship to this inevitable moment. It's the causal response to why you choose the way you choose and show up the way you show up. It's not a process of the mind. It's an alignment with the intelligence of your heart.

Therefore, choose to know what it is that you value most in life—right now—before proceeding further with this handbook. Because being clear about your values is a highly adept journey companion that will steward you towards living a life intentionally on purpose. Your answer will determine how you structure your life, how you journey through your days, and will influence your every decision.

Ask yourself again. "What do I value most in life?"

Your truest answer is your life as it's lived.

Live on purpose with clearly chosen values that serve you and the greater good.

> *"It's not hard to make decisions when you know what your values are."*
>
> —Roy Disney

Ends Values vs. Means Values

As you answered the previous question "What do I value most in life?" you may have found your answer to be something like "my children" or "my spouse" or "my house".

Here is an important distinction you need to consider.

Be sure you're clear about the difference between ends values and means values. Because valuing your house or your children or your family or your work are simply means to an end, not end values in themselves. You'll want to actively choose your end value. Again, ends values can be felt. They're a form of emotionally charged experience like love, gratitude, freedom, and joy.

Through your children, what value do you get to experience? Is it adventure? Is it love? Is it service? Children are tangible, they're "something". Values must match feelings. You can feel love of children. You can feel gratitude of children. You can't, however, feel children as a sponsoring value intention.

Many people will say, "I value money." Great. Now, what is it about money that you value? Does it give you freedom? Does it provide you with ample adventure? Does it supply you the feeling of security? Contribution? Abundance? Power?

For the purposes of this handbook, you needn't focus on the byproducts by which you experience a value, but the value itself that is felt, okay?

When you ask yourself, "What do I value most in life?" understand that it isn't a thing or a person. It's an emotion. It's a feeling. It's an experience you want to have through other than physical means.

Note to self...
  Ask yourself, "What do I value most in life?"
      As you choose, so too do you live.

Why Is Being Intentional Integral?

*I*f you were to pick up a dictionary right now, one of the definitions for the word "intent" would be paraphrased as, "an aim or a purpose." At its core, to be intentional means that you're living life on purpose.

Why is being intentional integral? Because life has no meaning save the meaning you give to it. If you're not living life intentionally, consider that somewhere you're lacking the vehicle necessary to live life on purpose. Without your event horizon, where might you end up along the journey?

Yet once you get clear, once you're at choice, and once you're intentional in your answer to the question "Who am I?" you literally become that answer, fully aware and completely conscious.

When you do this, you're living on purpose. You're giving your life direction. You're becoming who you choose to be, every moment, every day, and in every way imaginable.

> "Life is without meaning. You bring the meaning to it. The meaning of life is whatever you ascribe it to be. Being alive is the meaning."
>
> —Joseph Campbell

How to Remain Ever Intentional

*B*eing intentional is really quite natural. It's natural but not always normal. Because you've been the answer to every question you've ever asked, you already know, at some level, how to be intentional.

In those moments when you feel out of sorts, when there appears to be more unknowns than knowns, rely on your practices and processes to help steward you back into clearest choice intention. Being intentional is as simple as engaging the process by which you creatively choose to live a life worthy of you.

So, when you feel off, breathe, smile, feel grateful and increase your time in silence. Understand that you're the only one making IT up—LIFE as you choose to experience IT—so make IT up beautifully. That's the long and the short of learning how to be ever intentional.

A bit further in this handbook, you'll come to better understand the be-do-have paradigm, but for now, just know that to be intentional, the key is to BE IT. Choose who you desire to be. Then, allow your beingness to empower your actions. Act as someone who is being the experience acts. Withinasthru this simple process, you'll have all you ever desire to have.

Just don't be too surprised if you find your desire to accumulate "stuff" diminishes over time. Because as you get clearer and clearer that your truest work is in being and becoming the experience, you might come to find that having stuff is much less inspiring that it was earlier in your process.

Therefore, be conscious of your intentions, the intentions you ground withinasthru knowing who you are. Do you desire to be a supportive spouse and a contributing member of a happy family?

Are you Being a loving husband or wife in order to be congruent in sustaining your family?

Get very clear on who you desire to be, and then act on it by jumping into the river AS that. If it's difficult to BE that in the situation you've created at this moment, create a new situation or find new listening from different people. Act on your intention to BE IT by jumping into unknown situations and simply becoming that which you intend. Most of all, keep the constant idea in mind that you are making it all up. You are clearly at choice, intentionally choosing who you are. You are ever at choice in your life, at choice in your intentions.

> Note to self...
> Whatever you intend to experience...
> Just BE IT!

What Has to Occur WithInAsThru You for You to FEEL?

C onsider this, if you will. What has to occur withinasthru you in order for you to really feel the experience so deeply that it's unquestioning that you've felt it, you've become IT?

You've felt to the point where you were complete emotionally, mentally, spiritually, and physically with an experience at some point along your journey. Perhaps the birth of your children or your wedding day was such an integral experience? Possibly you've enjoyed experiences often referred to as "the zone" while playing sports—you know, that day the basket looked double its size, and just about every shot you took… swoosh!

In essence, you called forth experience through your own expression so rich in texture and so divine in its inspiration that it moved, touched, and inspired you back into an eternal answer of "Yes!" to What IS. And you flowed as river flows in this inevitable moment.

You've enjoyed at least a few of these precious moments in your life where everything moves into slow motion and your experience is complete and immersive.

If it's been a while since you've really felt, go back to childhood. Imagine the depth of emotion you had the first time you flew a kite, or you passionately played dress-up or race cars with your friends, or you rolled around on the ground with your first puppy. Go back to that feeling of complete abandonment, where time and worries and outside influences completely stopped and you were lost in a world of feeling.

What has to happen, then, for you to feel this again? What are your rules by which you allow yourself to receive the experiences you intend to receive? Ask yourself now. "What has to happen for me to feel?" "What are the rules by which I allow myself to experience my clearest values?" Then, consider aligning the rules such that they serve you rather than disserve you in your process.

Without feeling, your ability to be intentional is diminished. And the rules by which you allow yourself to experience the love or adventure, the joy or the freedom, the contribution or gratitude by which you desire to base your life on will determine whether your process is ease and flow as river, or filled with needless suffering. If you have a rule that says, "The world must be peaceful in order for me to feel peaceful," then you may never allow yourself to receive the experience of peace withinasthru.

Consider again this quote, "Seek not peace here, but find it everywhere." Knowing what you know right now, would you consider the possibility that this gift is simply a reminder to be the peace you seek in the world? Additionally consider that this is universally aligned no matter what value you seek to experience yourself as, no matter who you intend to be and become.

Feeling—that is being the experience you have chosen to be physically, emotionally, mentally and spiritually—is eternally important, because it's the magnet by which you attract your life as it is withinasthru you. How you're feeling is exactly what you're attracting to you right now. Get conscious of how you're feeling, be aware that the emotion you're feeling (gratitude, resentment, joy, or unhappiness) is bringing life in both form and experience to you exactly as you're feeling it. This is the power of your feelings.

> *"If it all just happens like this for the rest of my life, it's going to be one endless Groundhog Day. I determined that I was not prepared to submit to this regime, so I thought I had to do something about it."*
>
> —*Bruce Dickinson*

Note to self...

The more that you're aware of what your real feelings are, the greater your ability to respond being who you choose to BE.

Note to self...
Whenever you're off, choose to realign.
Remember to breathe.
Smile your knowingness.
Be grateful.

Live WithInAsThru Passion!

"Passion is the genesis of genius."
—Tony Robbins

R evisit your response, now, to what has to occur in order for you to feel. Take it deeper, all the way to your core, and ask yourself, "What ways of being allow me to feel the most passion?"

Remember the way you felt as a child when you played with abandon? Remember the last time you felt fully connected to the universe, where you utterly became one with IT, and lost yourself for an hour or a day, or even a second, without thinking about all that worries you—your bills, your job, your obligations, whatever?

Perhaps you've experienced it when you've written, or painted, or sung, or worked in the garden, or closed a multimillion dollar deal, or even played make-believe with your children. If you've been living a life of have-tos and grown-up lackluster obligations and routines, your passions may seem very far away.

But they're still there, percolating. Go deeper into the feeling of being who you are. Enter into thoughts of doing what makes you feel the most passionate. Now, consider the possibility that in order to have a life filled with passion, you must choose to be and live withinasthru passion.

Choose now who you desire to be and jump into that experience with the passion that emanates from within. The more you jump into being your passion, the more the universe will respond with expanding opportunities to experience yourself as passionate.

Ask yourself these questions again, "What gives me the most passion? What makes me feel most alive? What do I desire to experience that really makes me feel something, anything, more than I am feeling right now?"

You'll start to notice when your passion is taking over, when your life becomes a series of "get-tos" rather than "have-tos". Get excited to be who you are. Become enthusiastic about what you're getting to do, rather than what was, a moment ago, what you had to do, or where you had to go. In the moment you become your passion, you come to live withinasthru passion. As you choose to live with passion, all of your have-tos become get-tos, regardless of how they felt previously.

> *"Never let the odds keep you from pursuing what you know in your heart you were meant to do."*
>
> —*Satchel Paige*

Note to self...

Let your passion become your living joy.
Create your life to be a series of "get-tos" rather than "have-tos."

Note to self...
AND choose to live withinasthru passion.

why are you waiting?
what's the pause?
what's the hesitation?

be afraid no more,
of unknown tomorrows,
become more comfortable,
with what is unknown,
than what is known.

consider the known,
limitations to imagination,
that gift given you at birth,
to break all,
self-imposed limits.

What Are Your Habits of Comfort?

*I*t's important to be aware of where your habits of comfort are, because there's a distinct possibility that where you're comfortable, you're not experiencing life to its fullest. Where would you choose to live more often—in limitless possibility, or in limitation—in boundless choice, or in limited choice?

Perhaps change is a scary prospect for you, especially if you've made being comfortable your preferred intention. Often, you may get too comfortable with old patterns and become afraid to change.

What are your patterns of comfort? Do you watch television for hours every night, instead of investing your time in a project you're passionate about? Do you visit the same restaurants, the same grocery store, the same coffee shops, the same bars, simply because they're more comfortable than trying something new? How about new friends? When was the last time you met and made a new friend? Changed jobs? Or work? Or careers?

Whether or not comfort is bad isn't the question here. It's whether your comforts are serving or disserving you, serving or disserving the greater good. Nor is there a conversation contained here that suggests you let go of all worldly possessions or other such presumptuous language.

Consider, if you will, that once you seek to become more comfortable in the unknown than the known, you truly learn to break out of patterns that don't serve you or the greater good. More important is the possibility that by doing so, you become much more ready to express your ability to respond to this inevitable moment with greater resolve, more self confidence, increased clarity, enhanced choice and ever expanding personal power.

Be ever diligent in recognizing your patterns—especially the ones that are more muted and seemingly benign. When you recognize a habit of comfort, ask yourself the eternal question, "Does this really serve me? Does it serve the greater good?" If not, it's your moment to choose again, to get grateful for your ability to notice these patterns, honor them, and then make a new choice.

Consider choosing paths that embrace change. Choose to become more as you expand your personal power. And may you reflect the courageous vulnerability life asks you to embrace in order to be the ever changing being you are.

Change: A Different Perspective

Following is perhaps a different perspective on change. It's not the truth, nor is it a better perspective, it's simply another one...

Try adopting this new perspective to make change not only fun, but a useful tool in the process of choosing to live, on purpose, LIFE as you choose it to be.

Everything IS but one energy, and this energy is called LIFE. It is the individual and specific vibration of this energy that's referred to as its condition. Under certain conditions, certain things occur and appear to be what could be called true.

For instance, up is down and down is up—under certain conditions. The first astronauts uncovered a truth on an early trip to space—that definitions of "up" and "down" can simply disappear. Their truth changed, because the conditions of their experience changed.

Changing conditions create changing truth.

Truth is nothing more than a word meaning "what is so right now". A moment ago, science proved that the earth was flat. A moment before that, humanity proved that the Earth was the center of the universe. This was what was so then. Yet, what is so is always changing. Therefore, truth is always changing.

Your life consistently demonstrates that your truth is constantly changing too. It only takes a moment of reflection to get how your truth is in constant flux. What was your truth 6 months ago? How about when you were 6? When you were 12? When you were 21, what was your living truth back then?

Embracing change becomes simple when you consider this most basic observation—the process of life is always changing. LIFE IS change.

Life is a process; it's the place where you get to experience who you are and express it. Some might prefer the word evolution, the energy that shifts and evolves. Others are perhaps more poetic and see change as a river flowing, where one never witnesses the same river twice.

The core possibility contained in this consideration is to observe yourself as constant change, as well.

What time is it? Now. Where are you? Here. Again, ask yourself, "What time is it? Where am I?" Now. Here withinasthru this inevitable moment.

Seeing the inevitability of this moment is what allows you the ability to respond fully as who you are. As your ability to respond to this inevitable moment expands, so too does your ability to change and transform. With ever expanding responsibility, you become able to be the change you sought a moment before.

Because life is change—and you are but this part of LIFE that IS you—you are change. And as you learn to embrace change from the inside out, as who you are, you'll be increasingly able to create more powerfully, to choose withinasthru greater awareness, to settle less and less. You will choose to consciously live on purpose.

> *"If you want to be somebody else*
> *If you're tired of doing battles with yourself*
> *If you want to be somebody else*
> *Change your mind"*
> —Sister Hazel, "Change Your Mind"

What Are Your Strengths and Weaknesses?

Now is the time for you to take inventory, get to really know yourself. Understand yourself. Literally, imagine standing under yourSelf and taking a sweeping evaluation.

What are your strengths? What are your weaknesses?

You're probably very aware of what both of these are, as are those very close to you. Perhaps you're a whiz at accounting and financial maneuvering. Perhaps you're a prolific writer, natural at mothering, or an expert mountain biker. These strengths of yours, you know very well. They're probably what you enjoy doing the most, too.

But what are your weaknesses? Do you have a hard time handling money? Do you constantly fret about cleaning or household tasks? Do you have issues with grammar or spelling or a hard time expressing yourself to your loved ones? What are your weaknesses?

More often than not, where your weaknesses lie, that's where energy leaks occur in your life. So often, people let their strengths overcompensate for where they're weak, which leads to a very unbalanced life. Reshift yourself, then, to allow your strengths to encompass your weaknesses. If your weakness is food, find awareness in that, and then find a strength to compliment it. This will transform the weakness immediately.

How can you do this? Again, let's suppose your weakness is eating too much too often, but one of your strengths is your parenting abilities and your love of spending time with your children. Use this strength to go out, get more exercise with your children, learn about and utilize healthier eating plans for the entire family, and by default, your weakness will be diminished through your strength.

While you needn't be too radical and disciplined in the process of transforming your weaknesses into strengths, it's important to be aware of what serves you and what doesn't as you make this transition. Learning to balance these two important aspects of your personality will allow you to embrace change much more readily aligned with your clearest intentions.

> *"My weaknesses are my jumps."*
> —Oksana Baiul

Clear

Choice

Intention

Ask

Grateful

Giving

Receptive

Ask

What Does It Mean To Ask?

"Ask, and IT will be given to you."
"Knock, and the door will be opened."

*B*elieve it or not, the process of asking for what you desire is no more complicated than being willingness enough to ASK. Asking is exactly what you would imagine it to be. The gap in the process is usually not the asking, it's your willingness to ask in such a way that you know that what you ask for is granted. Set an intention, and ask the universe to fulfill your intention. The universe isn't picky, it isn't discriminating. It provides you with exactly what you ask for. But you must be willing to ask, willing to receive IT.

After you ask, simply trust and allow LIFE its process of giving you what you ask for. Then be willingness enough to receive IT. However, it is important that you have made a clear choice intention for what it is you're asking. Be clear in your request—precise yet with absolute abandon of the details. Let the universe handle the details. You have only to ask the universe with abandon and gratitude for what it is you truly desire.

So often, however, people will ask for something, someone, some experience, and then turn around to get caught up in the treadmill of their lives, forgetting that they've even asked in the first place. Asking is an ongoing, ever-changing thing. Be aware of what you're asking for at all times and on all levels, thought, word and action. Be clear in your thought process and the words that you use. Be conscious of any negative self-speak, because, again, LIFE knows only how to fulfill, not how to discriminate between that which you desire and that which you don't desire.

Become asking, from the deepest gratitude in your heart, knowing that you shall, if you're willingness enough, receive all that you ask for.

Know that the door is already open to you. Ask and IT is yours to receive. Receive IT.

> *"If your daily life seems poor, do not blame it;*
> *you have not been poet enough to call forth its*
> *riches; for the Creator, there is no poverty."*
> —*Rainer Maria Rilke*

Why IS Asking Integral?

Consider again that nothing in life is happening to you, your life, as you live it, exactly as it is, is occurring withinasthru you. This process is occurring withinasthru you exactly as you are choosing, whether you're conscious or not, aware or not.

While it may appear on the surface that you're being given things and experiences from LIFE without your directly asking, it is still occurring withinasthru you, just not at a conscious level.

Think about it this way. You are the only constant in your life, the only one. You're the only constant in every one of your relationships. You're the only one who has been in every one of your situations, circumstances, scenarios, and events. You bring in the people, the situations, and the circumstances of your life based upon your intention and attention; and you magnetize your life to you, exactly as it is through your feelings. Therefore, get clear that you're the only constant in your life. And get active in the process by which you're allowing your experience of life to occur withinasthru you. Be aware of what you're asking for.

Consider how living unaware and unconscious of this process has been working for you and not working for you. Perhaps if you pause and experience a little humility, you'll see with eyes wide open that you've likely had moments of pure joy, moments of boredom, with moments of anger and sadness mixed in with everything in between. And this is how everyone else is doing it, right? So it must be the way things are.

If instead you engaged the process of living on purpose by asking with clarity and intention, wouldn't you be able to bring forth that which you consciously want, rather than a default situation you may or may not have directly chosen had you been ever aware of the power of asking?

Asking is an integral part of the process to being, doing, and having all that you desire. It's the point in your personal power where you courageously ask for what you desire. It gives you the opportunity to weigh all options and choose the one that best serves you and the greater good. It allows you to laser-focus your clearest intentions into the ether, knowing the door is eternally open to your receptivity.

By consciously asking, you're setting into motion your life as you choose it to be—and perhaps you won't get what you ask for immediately, but you can be enveloped in gratitude, knowing that it's on its way.

> *"When a person really desires something, all the universe conspires to help that person to realize his dream."*
> —Paulo Coelho, "The Alchemist"

Note to self...

> Be willingness enough to ask
> for what you desire.
>
> Be able, willing and ready to
> receive what you ask for.

How Do You Ask?

*T*his question may seem to have an obvious answer, but there are distinctions to be made when you ask LIFE for an experience. First of all, become very focused on that which you desire. Know it. Feel it. Be grateful for it in advance.

As a consideration, be wary in your use of the word "want". When you're really in the "wanting" space, the universe will keep giving you exactly what you are asking for, namely, "wanting". It will most likely not give you the fulfillment of that which you otherwise claim you desire, but it might instead continue to give you experiences of wanting. Experiment with this one. There are no absolutes. Others use the word want with mixed results. Simply get clear about the words you use as LIFE matches intentions with results. It's up to you to be clarity in the way you ask, clear?

That's not to say that wanting is bad. Wanting always comes first. But choice is where you really get to utilize the power of asking. Come to the universal expression of choice, and ask. Ask with abandon, and ask with gratitude.

Offer to the universe, "I am loving. I am abundant. I am adventurous. I am healthy." In stating these choices, knowing that immediately your request is being answered, your becomingness is assured. You can let go in sheer, all-consuming appreciation. Smile your request home to your experience.

So, please ask in whatever way you feel most comfortable with. Ask in your silent time, as in a prayer. Ask out loud, in a room full of no one but you and your powerful creative source. Or, even more potent, ask in conversation with another. That which lives in conversation is already in existence. Engage your desires with the part of you that is your spouse, your friends, your family, or your coworkers to create magical conversation filled with infinite possibility.

Most importantly, ASK. Be ever asking, conscious of your desires, empowered with your ability to choose and clear in your intentions of who you are choosing to be and become.

> *"When you go to a club, you*
> *want everyone to dance.*
>
> *I'm just asking everybody to*
> *dance...enjoy this moment."*
> —Mary J. Blige

From Have, Do, Be...

C onsider this scenario: You desire to have a loving, caring, healthy relationship. You would like to be married. You've spent days and nights thinking about how much you crave this—how much having this will change your life into exactly what you desire.

You sit and lament about how lonely you are, how incomplete you are. How, if you just had the right man or woman in your life, you'd be able to do all of the things you think your life is lacking. You'd be able to be happy then, right? Once you had love, then you could do what you think people in love would do, and finally—finally—you'd be happy, full, and complete.

Sounds pretty familiar, doesn't it? The majority of humanity lives under this misconception. They try to direct their lives with the "have" coming first. It's a very easy way to put off ever becoming that which they desire, because until they first "have" something, they cannot experience the feeling or emotion or mental state that's truly motivating their desire.

Sadly, this misperception keeps you pretty stagnant in the long run. It allows you to live in inaction, thinking you're a victim of circumstance. Or you end up working far too hard to get "something" in order to feel "something," when there really is a much easier way. All you have to do is make a shift; shuffle around the words "have, do, and be," and you'll unlock one of the greatest gifts the universe has to offer.

In the example above, if you instead first intended to be loving, lovable and loved, you would invariably begin doing what someone who is loving, lovable and loved does. That is, you would be loving, lovable and loved by Self. This love would then be unable to be contained and you would then choose to share it with your friends, your family, your co-workers, and your neighbors.

You may find yourself becoming more social. Because after all, you can only give away that which you have to give, right? And who wants to be with someone needing to be loved? That's a recipe for disaster. It's a way to continued suffering and experiences of feeling loneliness.

When you focus on who you're choosing to be first, you'll do what a person who is being what you desire to be does. Having will become the byproduct of your beingness. Whether you've chosen to be happy, loving, adventurous or miserable, your choice will bring you the very experiences you seek in regards to what you desire to be.

> *"A boy used to ask his mother, 'How can I find the right woman for me?' and the mother would answer, Don't worry about finding the right woman—concentrate on becoming the right man."*
>
> —*Unknown*

WithInAsThru Self Love...

A never ending song,
when apart, together,
worlds connected,
experienced as One.

Loving others as Self,
sharing completely, without unspoken expectations,
understanding when it seems not understandable,
supporting, even when not in agreement,
listening without judgment,
working and growing, from many into One.

The dawn of each new day,
the promise of a brighter tomorrow,
hope of what can be,
willingness enough to choose it so,
hearts rhythmically beating,
one magnetic pulse home.

Giving and receiving,
a circle turned into infinity commitment,
learning from the losses that have come before,
letting go of what no longer serves,
healing all patterns of separation,
appreciating the differences,
while honoring traditions,
gratitude become certainty,
at cliff's edge,
jump time.

Understanding Self, understanding all others,
becoming change once sought external,
choosing "Just Us" way of seeing,
One humanity,
One LIFE,
ONE LOVE.

Self Love is all this and so much more,
growing like wild flowers in the fields of your tomorrow...
offered to you,
this inevitable moment.

Because you are loved,
more than words could ever hope to express,
know one thing—and this one thing do not doubt,
that as you choose to be ever loved, lovable and loving,
so too will you feel and experience an expanding Self love,
greater with each new sunrise,
than you did the day before...

...To Be, Do, Have

*M*ake the shift now, and you'll never turn back. Be at source in the matter of your life. Be at cause to what experiences you choose to call forth. Engage the be-do-have paradigm to your favor and you'll forever be glad you did. Allow this simple rule to guide the rest of your life, and you're well on your way to being, doing, and having whatever you desire, even as you learn to live life, as you choose it to be, on purpose, a role only you can perform..

So how do you do this?

> *"Ask not what the role can do for you; ask what you can do for the role."*
>
> —*Ricardo Montalban*

Immediately, right now, bypass all of the self-talk that's kept you thinking you can't experience what you desire until you have a certain thing. Shift from what you desire to have, to who you are choosing to BE.

Who do you desire to be? Do you desire to be abundance? Then start doing things that one who is abundant does. If someone needs a handout, remember, you're abundance. Fulfill. No matter what you think you have or don't have, know that through your actions you have more than what you perceive at this moment. Again, you can only give what you have to give.

The more you choose to become abundance, the richer experiences of abundance will arrive for you to experience yourself as abundant.

Action is the key to confidence. Confidence matched with your clarity and your heart gratitude is authentic power. It's the key to having that which you desire. Jumping directly into the river of action is the fastest and easiest way to make a shift in your life once you have chosen to BE IT first.

Remember: Being comes first. Feel yourself as being that who you desire to be. And Be It! Withinasthru you choice to BE IT, you will become it. Next, DO what you would do Being who you are being. Whether you've chosen to be abundant, or loving, or happy, let your beingness inspire your doingness. Again, jump into the experience with your whole self—whether you do it with people who are already in your life or new friends. After you realize how easy it is to BE and DO, then you will HAVE. And the having will seem almost effortless. It will arrive to you through amazing and miraculous channels. Be open and receptive.

Once you're really in the flow of BEingness, then everything becomes joy, unbridled expansion, and fun. Resist no longer what is, but BE first that which you desire. Just consider it. Experiment with this process. See how it works for you. Toss your negative self-talk and disbelief to the wind, if even for a moment.

To BE or not to BE? This is your eternal question. Who are you? Choose now. Be. Do. And you will, by default, have. And throughout it all, be eternally grateful, allowing gratitude to fill your every cell, your every thought, every moment you are.

Create your own miracles, starting today.

> *"I am my own experiment.*
> *I am my own work of art."*
> —*Madonna*

Note to self...
        Just BE IT!

Clear

Choice

Intention

Ask

Grateful

Giving

Receptive

Grateful

What does IT mean to BE Grateful?

"Gratitude is a powerful process for shifting your energy and bringing more of what you want into your life. Be grateful for what you already have, and you will attract more good things."

—Rhonda Byrne, *"The Secret"*

So what does it mean to BE grateful? Simply be grateful. Find every reason you can imagine to feel gratitude in your life, even if it's learning the gratitude in hard lessons learned. Be grateful ahead of time, when you've set forth a desire to the universe; be grateful for the knowingness that what you choose is already on its way to you.

To think, speak, and act upon inspired desires creates a burning passion to be something, to do something, to have something. Now add the ingredient of knowing. Add the certainty of gratitude. Because once you have a desire that you've asked for withinasthru thought, word, and action, there is no other prayer that matches intentions to experience more rapidly than a prayer of thanksgiving.

The more you learn to live in this place of certainty withinasthru gratitude, the more you'll choose to live with constant and ever expanding gratitude, a gratitude that is both intense and incredible. In short, that which you appreciate, appreciates.

"It is just that we should be grateful…"

—*Aristotle*

Note to self…

Gratitude, in advance, allows you
the experience of certainty.

Experiment with this. Be playful.

Practice Feeling Gratitude

A s you continue to engage the process of creating your life exactly as you desire and choose it to be, you'll find that you're living each day with greater gratitude for the people, the circumstances, and the events of your life.

Gratitude is the magical magnetic ingredient. It's the most powerful magnetic force imaginable. Use it knowingly. Bear its gift wisely.

Practice each day, through your three breaths and as often as possible, feeling gratitude for all the people, things, situations, and just the beauty of what IS.

Learning to live in gratitude will align your desires with your heart magnet, and bring to you your desires in ever increasing flow. Make time every day to fully feel gratitude, feel the ecstasy of all that you're creatively choosing your life to be.

> *"Any artist should be grateful for a grace which puts him beyond the need to reason elaborately."*
>
> —*Saul Bellow*

Note to self...   Breathe.

Smile.

Look up.

FEEL GRATEFUL for your
life exactly as IT IS.

Why IS BEing Grateful Integral?

Take a moment to imagine what you desire most—what circumstances, what situations, what experiences. Perhaps you desire a loving relationship. Imagine this relationship in detail. Desire it. Feel it. See it vividly in your mind. Ask the universe, out loud, right now, to bring this desire to you.

You could leave it at that. You could. And the universe would respond in its part. However, when you add gratitude to the mix, your power to create increases tenfold, perhaps even a hundredfold.

Do the exercise again. Imagine your desired experience exactly as before. Now, at the end, add gratitude. Let it fill your heart. Imagine exactly just how grateful you'd feel if you had that experience right now. Be grateful, because that experience is on its way to you, pulled ever more quickly by the gratitude you emanate.

While gratitude is an integral step in creating your life as you choose to live it, it's also integral to tending your garden, to re-aligning your magnet, and to clearing out any negating energy that may be repelling that which you desire.

Engage the power of neutrality when you begin blaming, complaining, or attacking. Engage the observer, and then find your gratitude. A moment before you may have been lost in a sea of confusion, but after you've taken three breaths and allowed gratitude to move in, you're clearer than you'd ever thought possible.

*"Grace is available for each of us every day—
our spiritual daily bread—but we've got to remember to ask for it with a grateful heart..."*

—*Sarah Ban Breathnach*

Note to self...

You are every moment you are.

For all that you are, BE grateful to Self.

Note to self...

**Your life becomes a masterpiece
withinasthru your Self Gratitude for IT.**

How to Remain Ever Grateful

*I*t may take practice remaining grateful, or it may be something that comes as second nature to you. Either way, as you begin to tend your garden, as you remember, daily, to do your three breaths when your magnet feels off, the habit of gratitude will become your primary way of living, of seeing and of listening.

Spend time in silence every day, experience the IS at its purest level. That will help you shift into remaining ever grateful. Remember, you're a walking, talking magnet, and the more you get grateful for that which you desire, the more you attract your desires at an ever quickening pace.

With a radiant smile full of effervescent light, let gratitude become your primary state of being. Let it consume you. Allow your gratitude to become your certainty—in every situation and every moment you are.

Note to self...

Just BE Grateful!

FEEL gratitude in your every heartbeat...

The Power of Your Heart

*T*hat which you appreciate, appreciates. This is the power of your heart. Your feelings are what attract to you infinite possibilities of experience and expression. Honor your feelings. Act on them. Make them more prominent, and bring them forth more often in as many ways as you are willing.

As you begin to do this, you shift your magnetic abilities. Your heart will send forth your request to the universe based on the power of your feelings.

HeartMath, a cutting edge company dedicated to studying the power of the heart, has scientifically measured an electromagnetic field that extends spherically from your heart outward.

> "The electromagnetic field generated by the heart envelops the entire body and extends out in all directions into the space around you. The heart's electromagnetic field is by far the most powerful field produced by the body and can be measured many feet away for you by using sensitive devices."
>
> —Doc Childre, Founder of HeartMath,
> "The HeartMath Solution"

Given that there is but one energy, one information and one intelligence that is all of LIFE, it's possible to consider that this heart field is what connects you to infinite intelligence. This is very important work being done by Doc Childre and his exceptional team of professionals. To learn more about HeartMath, please check on the resources center at *http://www.WithInAsThru.com/thehandbook/resources.*

Imagine a spherical energy field emanating from your heart that pulsates pure possibility. Your feelings, especially the feeling of gratitude, attract energy, information, and intelligence from this field of infinite possibility. Now imagine each possibility as a string of electric lightning that connects you to this inevitable moment you are—attracting the exact combination of energy, information, and intelligence to you as an experience for you to be who you are and to experience yourself as this.

Incredibly, gratitude is the one emotion that significantly increases the power of this electromagnetic field. As you sync your body into gratitude, as you come into coherence, you literally become that which you're being grateful for. You attract life, as you live it, withinasthru you; and gratitude is the essential ingredient by which you attract what you desire to experience, life as you choose it to be. It really is this simple.

But now, for a moment, imagine these spherical electromagnetic fields emanating from each human you come into contact with. There is always a place, then, where you become one with those around you. There is a place where your heart fields meet to conjoin in universal unity. This is the true magic of shared space-time. It's the science behind the statement, "you become who you surround yourself with." The energy, information, intelligence that is you is enmeshed and immersed with the energy, information and intelligence of who you share this inevitable moment with.

Indeed, it's been proven that after sitting or standing close to another person for a small length of time, your hearts begin to beat in synchrony. Consider how powerful this is when you receive it at an even deeper consideration.

You impact those around you by simply just BEing who you're choosing to be at any given moment. Who would you choose to be, then? How would you choose to show up? Will you show up differently now knowing that you have such an impact upon your friends, family and loved ones, withinasthru your beingness? Will you more carefully choose who you share space and time with?

> *What if LIFE on this Earth,*
> *Humanity's evolutionary promise,*
> *IS Occurring,*
> *WithInAsThru this part of LIFE that IS you?*
> *Who would you choose to BE?*
> *Would you BE Willingness Enough,*
> *To BE IT?*

The power of your heart is magnificent and potent. Use it wisely. Exercise it joyfully, and draw upon it withinasthru gratitude. It will change your life, and the lives of those close to you.

As you change your heart, so too do you change the world.

> *"You will recognize that you are the inviter, the creator, and the attractor of all things that come to you; and you will, indeed, then have deliberate control of your own life experience."*
> —Esther & Jerry Hicks, "The Law of Attraction"

reflections of every moment you are,
withinasthru you,
this inevitable moment,
a walking, talking magnet,
you are,
LIFE,
as you choose IT,
IT IS.

Walking, Talking Magnets

Consider the implications of this thought: You are a walking, talking magnet. Perhaps this is a clearer model to employ the processes offered in this handbook? Everything you are, do, and say—everything you feel, every response you have—simply serves to attract more of what you're being, feeling, doing, and saying.

You can use this awesome power consciously or unconsciously. Perhaps, you've been using it unconsciously for the majority of your life. But what would you choose? How would you prefer to go about living? Would you rather spend it unconsciously attracting that which you no longer desire? Or would you rather, moment-by-moment, day-by-day, consciously create your reality with your magnetism set to bring you that which you desire?

When your magnet is off, how do you know it's off? How do you know it's set to attract that which you don't desire, instead of that which you do? You know because you're able to observe the observable. You're off whenever you're blaming, complaining, explaining, justifying, attacking, or defending. When you monitor yourself doing any of these things, that's when you know it's you, you're the one "off". Through awareness, you can consciously shift. Make the shift as often as is necessary to get back to feeling gratitude and you'll engage the magnetic qualities of your heart field to bring your desires home.

The best way to go about realigning your magnet, then, is to do your daily practices. Get silent. Get aware. And, most importantly, forgive any perceived trespasses, and then get expansively grateful for what is.

*"Our lives become beautiful not because we are
perfect. Our lives become beautiful because we
put our heart into what we're doing."*
                                                —Sadhguru

No matter what it looks like in the world of duality, in the world
of illusion, you are that you are. If your magnet feels off, remember, forgiveness and gratitude. It's an amazing realization, every
time you choose it, because it literally lightens you up. It's been
written in poems and stories throughout the ages, the moment
of "lightening" by forgiveness and gratitude. And after you get
to that point, you simply start letting things occur withinasthru
you effortlessly.

Using your inherent ability as a walking, talking magnet allows
infinite spheres of possibilities. Tend your garden, live in neutrality, realign your magnet, and nothing will be impossible for you
to be or become. You'll have unlimited access to experience the
richness and depth of life.

*"Take one step towards Allah, Allah will take
10 steps towards you. Walk towards Allah, and
He will run towards you."*
                                        —Islamic Teaching

Practice Allowing Gratitude
to Become Your Certainty

*C*elebrate and enjoy all that you create, have created,
withinasthru your life, lived. Whatever is now occurring withinasthru you, own it, claim it, thank IT! To
reject any part of IT is to reject a part of Self.

If there is some aspect of creation you find you no longer enjoy, thank it and begin the next process with a new desire, a new thought, a new word, your next action. Simply choose again. Request the next fulfillment to your desire. And this circle continues withinasthru your entire life, exactly AS IT IS occurring WithInAsThru yoU.

Trust and allow your gratitude to be your certainty, knowing and being thankful for all that you create. From this, you'll be ever closer to living your dreams true and experiencing your every desire fulfilled spontaneously.

When you ask the universe for an experience, when you find yourself wishing aloud, be grateful immediately. Let that gratitude fill you up with such certainty that you know there could be no other way than what you desire.

Practice it now. Embrace it. Think of what you desire while expanding your feelings of gratitude. In this gratitude, you won't need to wait. Patience will become an antiquated experience. You will just live in blissful knowing that which you've asked for is already on its way to your experience.

Gratitude is your certainty. It leaves no "ifs". It leaves no "whens". It only leaves a peaceful knowing that you're the creator of your life, exactly as IT IS. What more experimentation would you request for you to choose to practice this gratitude as often as is necessary to become IT?

Note to self...

Experiment no more.
Just BE IT withinasthru Gratitude
as your Certainty.

Clear

Choice

Intention

Ask

Grateful

Giving

Receptive

Giving

What Does IT Mean To BE Giving?

Y ou are the key, the only key, to your life as IT IS because your life IS occurring withinasthru you. So, the only possible way to gain additional "keys" is to get that you're IT; you're every key you would imagine you seek.

Have you, at least in moments, noticed that while the players of your life may have changed, as have the circumstances, events, situations and scenarios, you've been the only constant? The only one.

This has been repeated often in this handbook because of its integral importance. Therefore, giving becomes easy when you realize that what you give, whether it's love or anger, abundance or stinginess, you can only give to another what you have to give. And no matter who you choose to give to—be it your loved ones or to strangers—you are simply giving to Self.

Giving is being in service; it's following the extended Golden Rule:

> *"Do unto others as you would have done unto you,*
> *Because there is none other than you.*
> *Give unto others as you would have given unto you,*
> *Because there is none other than you."*

Remember that, and you'll be ever more willing to give. Giving is ultimately an elevated state that, when you understand the concept of "ask and it shall be given," gets you into service to others. It helps you realize that you have never lacked that which you desire—that your lack has simply been an illusion perpetuated by misunderstanding. A misunderstanding that you could desire something that you're not already.

*"I try to make my life about service, and hope
that one day we can all 'see' a little better because God is… everyone and everywhere."*
—Russell Simmons

Give, then, what you would receive, and what you would receive WILL be received exponentially and with magnificent
abundance.

Why IS Giving Integral?

Τ he quickest and easiest way to receive that which
you desire is to first become grateful for it, then
give it away to the best of your abilities. There's
no need to wait—you can start giving immediately. Choose to
be in service right now.

Would you desire to experience yourself as greater abundance?
Give to those who show up to offer you the experience of being
abundance. Immediately, you have the experience of being abundance; in your gratefulness for this abundance and your choosing
to express your abundance withinasthru service, more will come
your way, effortlessly.

Would you desire to experience yourself as love? Give love away,
unabashedly and with passion. Smile at everyone you meet, embrace your friends and become love to all who surround you. Love
will come to you, then, in great waves because you are BEing love.
Your magnet of love is set withinasthru your very being.

Get into service right now, wherever you see a need and wherever
you find your desires. Become creative with your giving—the universe loves creativity. As you give, so shall you receive. Without
giving, without being and doing that which you desire, your

magnet remains weakened. You will remain in an idea of lack, when the universe knows nothing but abundance.

Giving is integral because once you begin giving, you'll see avalanches of your fulfilled desires flowing your way.

How to Remain Ever Giving

*N*ow this may seem remedial. But it's important to add this reminder to this conversation. Unfortunately, this often becomes a game of manipulation, like somehow the universe doesn't know your real motives in giving.

When you give withinasthru your willingness to give, you communicate to the universe your enoughness. You're not giving merely to receive. That would be an empty action that will not sustain your desires. Yet when you choose to truly give as an expression of who you are, so too do you receive ever expanding experiences to be who you are. And it becomes easier and easier to remain giving.

Apply the extended Golden Rule, and you begin to realize that whenever you give, you're literally giving to yourself—this part of you that is "other". The faster you get into service to others, the more you're able, willing, and ready to receive. As well, the more you give, the more abundant you become in that which you give.

Imagine two puppies. One is silent, withdrawn and gives nothing to its owners. The other is loving, caring, happy and full of life. Which one is going to receive more love in reciprocity? The puppy that gives love in abundance will receive even more love to experience, won't it?

And so too is it with you. If you desire to be happy, give happiness to everyone around you. If you desire abundance, start giving the abundance you are to whomever shows up to allow you the experience of being abundance.

Go to wherever you know there are those in need, show up with a pocket full of ones or even fives, and just start giving. Remember that no matter how much your money means to you, it means so much more to the person who's receiving it. Now, this isn't meant to tell you to give all your money away. To put yourself in absolute need would serve the opposite objective. But give more than is initially comfortable. Stretch. Express your abundance. And through this, you'll have the experience and expression of abundance in ever expanding ways.

The fastest way to shift a pattern is to jump into the new experience you desire to have. There is no faster way to shift a pattern than to jump into the experience of it as that which you're giving away, that which you're in service to another for. If you desire peace, then the faster you can BE peace in relationship to another, the more you're able to express yourself as peace. The more you choose to be peaceful, the more peace exists in every moment you are.

If you're ready for more, you will have no problem giving more. You will be ready to receive it in multitudes more than you give it. Give and give and give, until you understand that what you're giving is what you're ready, willing, and able to receive.

Note to self...
Giving and receiving are one experience.
Together they form a complete circle.

Beauty withinasthru beauty,
Choice withinasthru choice,
You get to choose how you SEE the world.
As you choose to see IT, so IT IS,
Where Seer, Seen and Scenery,
Are One.

Clear
Choice
Intention
Ask
Grateful
Giving
Receptive

Receptive

What Does IT Mean To BE Receptive?

*I*n the state of consciousness you're in at this moment, you may have difficulty with the concept of receiving. "How could I not receive that which I ask for?" you might ask.

Imagine what you most desire. No doubt, within your imagining, you've probably set up obstacles to receiving it. If you desire more wealth, perhaps you think you have to do "this" or "that" first in order to receive it. Or perhaps you believe you won't receive it if certain planets aren't aligned just right. Perhaps you've lived with a belief all your life that "money doesn't grow on trees," so you think receiving it in the way you envision is simply impossible.

What is receptivity? What does it mean to be receptive? It's your ability, your willingness, and your readiness to receive that which you ask for. Your only job, in this inevitable moment, is to trust and allow the universe, LIFE itself, to do its magic and perform its function—to give to you what you ask for and then be receptive to receive IT.

> "A very receptive state of mind—not unlike a sheet of film itself—seemingly inert, yet so sensitive that a fraction of a second's exposure conceives a life in it."
>
> —*Minor White*

Note to self...

Once you ask for IT withinasthru Gratitude as your Certainty, BE willingness enough to receive IT.

Why IS BEing Receptive Integral?

G iving and receiving is a circle. In order for one to experience giving, another must be receiving.

Receiving is integral to the process and appears to be where many slide off track. However, as you clear yourself of your patterns of separation, you'll become more ready and willing to receive. Because once you ask for something and allow gratitude to be your certainty, then you must be willingness enough to receive what you ask for, or you'll never allow yourself the experience you called forth.

Often you'll claim the process doesn't work because you've yet to allow yourself to receive and have challenges receiving. Be aware of how you receive from others. Do you receive graciously or are you uncomfortable receiving what others desire to give you?

Say this aloud, "I am a great giver and an excellent receiver." How did saying this make you feel? Did it make you feel strong or uncomfortable? Whether gifts or acknowledgement, you may not be as receptive as you might have hoped. Awareness of this pattern will help you to source the cause of your unwillingness.

> "Each day offers us the gift of being a special occasion if we can simply learn that as well as giving, it is blessed to receive with grace and a grateful heart."
>
> —Sarah Ban Breathnach

Being an excellent receiver is integral to the process of creating life as you chose it to be.

Note to self...
    Receive well.

How to Remain Ever Receptive

*M*ost people have very little problem giving—it's receiving that gets in the way of truly manifesting their desires. Say this to yourself, right now and as often as necessary, "I am a great giver, and an excellent receiver." Feel it as you say it.

Did you take pause at the receiving part? Was that a little difficult to truly feel? Say it again. "I am a great giver, and an excellent receiver." Continue to say this until you feel it, believe it, and know it to be who you are.

All of your perceived suffering comes from your resistance to what is. So what part of receiving are you resistant to? Once you begin to live in gratitude, and once you tend your garden properly, your ability to receive will be greatly enhanced.

Then once you become giving, once you understand that giving and receiving are one in the same, abundance in whatever form you desire will flow to you with ease—and you'll receive it with open arms, grateful for its now arrival.

If you no longer resist what is, you'll start allowing IT to be exceptional, whatever experience you have asked for. And by allowing IT to be exceptional, IT IS exceptional. There are no ordinary moments. By allowing what you have asked for to exceed even your wildest imagination, your wildest imagination will be exceeded.

> *"There is a truth deep down inside of you that has been waiting for you to discover it, and that truth is this: you deserve all good things life has to offer."*
>
> —Rhonda Byrne, *"The Secret"*

Note to self...
Remain open and willing to
receive what you ask for.

Be responsible to receive your desires
into experience and you'll live a life rich
with experience—a life worthy of you.

Practice Giving and Receiving Fresh Seeing & Listening

"Choose to live, work and play where you're celebrated, not where you're tolerated."

—Matt Bacak

Have you ever walked into a moment where someone's seeing or listening of you outdated who you are? Perhaps you came home for the holidays only to be seen and listened to as the little brother; and then to your amazement you actually find yourself feeling and acting your decades-ago role?

This is a normal reality in most family situations. It is also a pattern in many of your friendships and work environments because giving and receiving new seeing and fresh listening to those you're most close to can be very challenging. Yet, the seeing and listening you give and receive is integral to your process of consciously evolving.

"If you have not seen your brother for 3 days,
look closely; know he has changed.
If you have not seen him for 3 weeks,
forget who you knew; meet him again."

From a different perspective, have you ever enjoyed one of those moments where you walked into a seeing and listening that catapulted you into a new possibility of what it means to be you? Perhaps you were invited to deliver a key note address, or it may have been a new lover's eyes that intoxicated you into choosing a new way of showing up? Regardless of the source, when you received fresh listening and seeing, did it not help you in transforming yourself quickly?

Moments like this are true gifts. They allow rapid growth and the expression of personal power. Such a moment can only be described as fresh. It renews you. It brings you back to the beginning again where all possibilities exist. It's an opportunity to recreate yourself anew and to represent yourself as this new you that you have now glimpsed.

This is the magic of opening and expanding into purpose-filled community. This is the miracle that arrives when you fully show up in moments, willing and ready to be the you beyond your roles and identities. Because when you do, you too will be in a space to receive the fresh listening and seeing that can catapult you into ever-expanding tomorrows.

As you learn how to re-present yourself, fully showing up, you'll more easily give others the fresh listening and seeing they can use to help them transform as well.

Giving and receiving seeing and listening is a circle because as you see so too are you seen. As you listen, so too are you listened to. The more you learn to give fresh listening and seeing, the more you'll be willing and able to arrive into moments withinasthru the gift of transformation, yours and others.

Receive this fresh seeing, this inspired new listening. And be willingness enough to provide it to yourself as often as is necessary to give yourself permission to change. Because as you give yourself permission to change, so too do you give this fresh seeing and listening to those who come upon your path, requesting it.

As you give to it others, so too do you give it to the world. Choose to give and receive fresh listening and seeing often and freely and you'll bring to life every possibility you've ever imagined possible.

> *"Change the way you look at things,*
> *the things you look at change."*
> —*Wayne Dyer*

As you begin to adapt this practice into your daily way of being, you'll come to really see that as you shift your seeing and listening, so too do you shift the way people see and listen to you. All of a sudden, as you're seeing and listening, so too are you seen and heard. And in moments, you'll get glimpses where you get that the seer, the seen, and the scenery are one.

Notice then the patterns of the way in which you choose to see and listen to those you are closest to. Be willing to give the fresh seeing and listening you desire to receive. As you give it, be willing to receive it. Because the Golden Rule is one of the clearest stewards ever given—see and listen to others as you would choose to be seen and listened to, because there is none other than you.

Seek not peace here, but find it everywhere. Seek not love here, but find it everywhere. As you listen, you do so because of how you see. You see as a result of who you are being. As you see and listen then, so too do you know. As you know, you're able to trust. As you trust, you invoke the possibility of love.

Who you're choosing to be in this inevitable moment determines the seeing and listening you're able to give and receive. This is how it is that as you are, so too IT IS. But change the way you look at things, as a result of a new choice about who you are being, and the things you look at change. The words you hear shift. What you know transforms. Your ability to trust expands. Allowing you to trust things to be as they are, not as you want them to be, you're now able to trust others to be who they are, not as you once expected or needed them to be. As you trust, you enable love. As you love, so too are you loved. Only now is the experience of unconditional love possible.

There are few gifts you'll ever give or receive that will serve you and others as fully as fresh listening and seeing.

Note to self...

Practice giving fresh seeing and listening to every moment you are, and you will come to see that there truly are no ordinary moments.

Shared Process, Shared Purpose, Shared Hope...

A great teacher once said, "My entire life's work is inspired by my desire to receive just one more glimpse of the divine IS." This is important for you to consider. It is an important thought to reflect upon. Its greatest gift, should you allow yourself to receive its wisdom, will save you years of needless suffering and hardship. Allow the words to penetrate your BEing.

Get that there IS no thing that ever was, is, or will be said or written that hasn't already been said or written in some form.

There IS no thing that you're ever going to do that hasn't already been done. Therefore, there is no thing in existence that doesn't, in some form of energy, information, intelligence, already exist WithInAsThru yoU.

Thus, free yourself from false importance. Clear your mind from wanting needless praise. Stop seeking ego's gratification of approval or recognition from others. Explode your self-imposed limitations back into the nothingness from which they've arrived.

You can live this free. It is your destiny. It is the very promise of your humanity. Just get that you're a unique thread of existence, intertwining all that's ever been said or done, all that was, is, or will ever be. Not the you that still craves importance, approval, or recognition, but the yoU that gets—truly gets—that there's a purpose, a promise, only you can fulfill.

And it's a purpose worthy of you. It's a life lived on purpose, filled with passionate love and effervescent service. Life can be fun, and it can be fun with limitless possibilities.

Allow your clarity to be your confidence. Let gratitude be your certainty. Live on purpose, LIFE as you choose IT to BE. Your work, if you will, is to expand the very possibility of what it means to BE human.

As you are, so too IS humanity Being and BeComing. And it's time for all of you, as humanity, to jump into the next phase of your evolutionary promise. It truly is jump time.

> *"We all have the extraordinary coded within us, waiting to be released."*
>
> —Jean Houston

You're alive at this exact moment to participate in humanity's jump into its next evolutionary expression. What larger inspiration is there than to be your unique, celebrated expression of LIFE? Trust your imagination to be your architect. Imagination is ever so much more important than knowledge as a catalyst to humanity's evolution.

*"Because throughout the evolution of humanity,
ALL have been called.
It's just that very few have been willingness enough to
choose Self.
Will you choose Self when called?
Consider this moment your call to choose Self."*

Be then a voice to this inspired evolutionary thought. Be willingness enough, knowing and trusting that you've been preparing your whole life—lifetimes, even—to BE HERE NOW, in this inevitable moment, infinite possibilities, you at pure choice.

Practice this in your relationships. Practice BEing this in your roles as mother, as father, as husband, as wife, as friend, as brother, as sister, as fellow co-creator of LIFE as IT IS. Practice BEing this in your work, in your businesses, in your art, your music, your poetry, your dance, your every movement. Practice BEing this withinasthru every moment you are. And so IT will BE ever more reflected withinasthru humanity's experience on Earth.

Regardless of the messenger by whom this message arrives, get now that whether or not this message is true doesn't matter. What matters is whether this message serves you and the greater good. Does it move you to action? Does it touch you to feel new possibilities? Does it inspire your very being? If not, ignore it. If yes, apply its message to your living wisdom and choose to choose Self.

"Love is my religion."
—Ziggy Marley, "Love Is My Religion"

Every word written in this handbook lives withinasthru you or it couldn't exist in any moment you are. Regardless of the implications of this statement, BE honoring of your own unique process. Live life one breath, one step at a time upon your journey into the boundless.

Be gentle with your process, even as your process is eternally intertwined withinasthru humanity's evolutionary process. As you learn to apply the knowledge offered within the pages of this handbook, you'll become wise, no matter where you are this moment. Consider this process as you would any of your processes, no more and no less complicated than learning to ride a bike.

Before you saw another riding a bike, you didn't even know that you didn't know how to ride. Then, immediately upon seeing another riding, you too desired to ride, even as you became aware that you didn't know how to ride.

When you got on your first bike, like most others, you had training wheels. Your training wheels here are just to experiment with the concepts offered. Then, simply consider the ideas and begin to apply them to your life as you will.

The only way you learned how to ride a bike was by learning how not to ride it, right? And no matter how many times you fell down, you got back up, didn't you? Therefore, be gentle with yourself. Keep getting back on the bike regardless of how many times it feels like the ideas don't work. Because the more you get back in the seat, the more you remember yourself as one who knows how to ride.

How about today? Is riding a bike difficult at all? Of course it isn't. No more than driving a car is, and let's not pretend that you were a totally competent driver the first day behind the wheel. Yet, today you can drive with one knee while you eat a sandwich with one of your hands and talk on your cellular phone with the other, can't you? Even if such driving is unsafe, you are confident in your knowing that you are a driver.

And so it is with life. Withinasthru your choice to apply the knowledge in this handbook, there may be a learning curve experienced as either resistance or catharsis.

Whenever or however the upheaval may occur withinasthru you, as you learn to apply the knowledge here into your living wisdom, let the learning process be no different than riding a bike or driving a car. For the purposes of this handbook, come to refer to any aspect of perceived suffering of this learning curve as "evolutionary catharsis". Evolutionary catharsis occurs when you push yourself to make different choices, new changes in order to be, do, and experience a life lived on purpose, a life lived exactly as you choose it to be.

It's important to additionally consider that without evolutionary catharsis there is no growth, no expansion of awareness, no evolution. Catharsis is, in fact, the proof that evolution is happening, that the process is working, that you are expanding and realizing your dreams true. This is true in relationship to you and your life, as well as to the jump time humanity is experiencing today.

It has been, and will continue to be, a fascinating journey where each breakthrough is more amazing and fulfilling than the last. Your catharsis need not be painful. It is not necessary to suffer at all. However, because you are the creator of your every experience withinasthru your willingness to feel what is emotionally present for you, you may still default to old patterns of drama and suffering. Instead of relying on old patterns of separation, release any and all blame, complain, explain, attack, and defense patterns by remembering that even your perceived suffering is occurring withinasthru you, okay?

Because you are always at choice, use the following consideration to help you weather any perceived storm.

> *"In the moment it appears that it is all falling apart, it is really all falling back together again at the next highest level... not just more, or better, or different... a transformation from withinasthru you that wasn't even possible before your choice to expand, to grow, to become, this moment you are."*

Read the above consideration again. It's this important. It's a key reminder that you'll come to rely on from time to time as you move deeper into the complete experience you are.

Create this moment, then, as a new beginning. Choose now to be an awakening to the enfoldment of your soul's desire to live passionately on purpose with joy and abundance.

Use this handbook as a sling-shot, no longer getting needlessly trapped in the cycles of drama or the relentless pursuit of needing to be right. Instead, simply get that you're evolving, growing, and becoming. Any catharsis that occurs withinasthru you, or is reflected in your world, is part of the process.

IT IS What IS. And many of the friends that you've come to love, appreciate, and grow with may not choose to join you withinasthru this most critical moment of your growth. They may not celebrate your choice to live more fully, as you might expect. They may even say things that hurt or cause you pain. Feel it, but refuse to wear their limitations any longer. Refuse to engage further the patterns of suffering that encircle you back to the dramas and misery that represents so much of what it meant to be in relationship with them.

Be the eye of the storm, the cause of the chaos, the stillness inside the tornado as well as the ever encompassing winds of change… breathing and smiling, seeing and knowing this moment as the gift that will take you into your chosen tomorrows.

Know this IS so.

And so IT IS.

One Additional Consideration, If You Will…

The greatest opportunity of your time is that every problem that exists, exists because you give IT existence. You're its cause of appearance and, thus, its only source of disappearance. Every problem that exists today for humanity, humanity is both the cause of and the solution to. This is the greatest gift you can receive from this living consideration.

The true power of humanity is that the opportunity to transform all of space and time, the opportunity to be response-able for IT ALL lives forever in your willingness to change the only part of space and time in your absolute influence. Your self.

To this end, get clear. Release any and all patterns of separation. Live at conscious choice. Be intentional with your clearest values. Ask to be the change you a moment ago sought externally. Allow gratitude to be your certainty. Give what you most desire to receive. Be willingness enough to receive IT in return.

Know that you know that nothing in life is ever happening to you. Your life as an individual, LIFE as experienced on Earth, IS Occurring WithInAsThru yoU, withinasthru humanity.

Humanity's evolutionary promise has now arrived withinasthru your willingness enough to BE the change you most desire to experience as LIFE on Earth.

Live on purpose, LIFE as you choose IT to BE.
As you live, so too shall IT BE.
Ashea.

A. S. Kurslf

LIFE as You Choose IT to BE...

So few times, it seems to be, okay, for you to simply BE.
So well orchestrated this illusion is...
it draws you in and keeps you separate.

You forget sometimes Who You Really Are,
forgetting, in moments, just how far you've come.

It's there sometimes in your eyes,
that faint memory of time gone by...

But isn't tomorrow, yesterday for some;
and isn't today already come, already gone?

Let love mend what you perceive to be broken,
you have after all, remembered to show up,
this inevitable moment.

Receive the receivable, choose Self once again.

Yes, you've gone through a lot,
everyone's burden the heaviest,
just ask 'em.

You've made whole the realities you came to experience,
every person upon journey pre-sent to assist,
from loved ones to perceived enemies,
each played their role to perfection,
allowing you opportunities to experience Self,
in relationship to that part of you, them.

Choose love now to guide you in your every creation,
take this love sown deep into your heart,
to build your life upon the bedrock,
of its most unconditional form.

While many days may pass without perhaps a simple,
"thank you," said,
and it might all too often appear
as though others really don't care,
please remember, especially during cold moments felt alone,
the warm blanket of knowing,
it's all occurring withinasthru you.

The you that you share,
IS your recipe for how IT shows up,
as you choose to experience your truth,
your choices become you.

Every feeling felt comes around full circle,
returning to you what you feel to be so.

Be grateful,
let your full love shine bright,
you're a child of LIFE,
a Being of Light.

Be this light unto darkness,
illuminating full the nothingness,
from which you've arrived.

Receive every creation crafted,
your reflections in perpetual mirrors.

One choice eternal,
to accept IT or suffer IT.

May you arrive again and again,
to accept IT,
as every moment you are.

Each reflection serves to remind,
you are as special as you choose to BE,
here as a cog caught in a system of insanity,
or one who lives on purpose,
a role only you can perform.

Trust your willingness to guide you,
feeling your way,
as you Will.

As you are,
IT IS.

LIFE as You Choose IT to BE!

WithInAsThru yoU!
The Letters

www.WithInAsThruYou.com
subscribe@withinasthru.com

Contribute to the
A. S. Kurslf Collaborative

The idea is simple. To create, in as many ways as is possible, reminders to those who have not quite remembered to ask Self.

The Collaborative is seeking poets, musicians, rappers, artisans, business people, government representatives, scientists, religious leaders, philanthropists…anyone willingness enough to give their inspiration practiced in such a way as to move, touch, and inspire others to ask Self.

For more information and to add your name to the Collaborative:

www.ASKurslfCollaborative.com
(888) ASK-SELF